"There are signs here and there across the sion for a just, participatory, and sustainabl new stirring and clarifies directions in which it will express itself. In part ... fills the promise of feminism that as women are fully incorporated into the leadership of the church, ways of thinking and acting will also change. These chapters lure us into new forms of society more than they condemn us for our present failures."

—John B. Cobb Jr., Professor Emeritus, Claremont School of Theology

He has told you, O mortal, what is good;
and what does the L*ORD require of you*
but to do justice, and to love kindness,
and to walk humbly with your God?

—Micah 6:8

TO DO JUSTICE

A Guide for Progressive Christians

Rebecca Todd Peters
Elizabeth Hinson-Hasty
EDITORS

Westminster John Knox Press
LOUISVILLE • LONDON

Book design by Sharon Adams
Cover design by Lisa Buckley

First edition
Published by Westminster John Knox Press
Louisville, Kentucky

This book is printed on acid-free paper that meets the American National Standards Institute Z39.48 standard. ♾

PRINTED IN THE UNITED STATES OF AMERICA

08 09 10 11 12 13 14 15 16 17 — 10 9 8 7 6 5 4 3 2 1

Library of Congress Cataloging-in-Publication Data

To do justice : a guide for progressive Christians / Rebecca Todd Peters, Elizabeth Hinson-Hasty, editors. — 1st ed.

p. cm.

Includes index.

ISBN 978-0-664-23282-5 (alk. paper)

1. Church and social problems—United States. 2. Religion and politics—United States. I. Peters, Rebecca Todd. II. Hinson-Hasty, Elizabeth L.

HN39.U6T6 2008

261.8—dc22

2007052505

Contents

Contributors

Gloria H. Albrecht is Professor of Religious Studies (Ethics) at the University of Detroit Mercy and an ordained minister in the Presbyterian Church (U.S.A.). Her work focuses on issues of economic justice as seen through the lens of women's work. Her most recent book, *Hitting Home: Feminist Ethics, Women's Work, and the Betrayal of Family Values*, critiques the antifamily norms of current business practices and the neoliberal economy.

Elizabeth M. Bounds is Associate Professor of Christian Ethics at Emory University. She works with peacemaking and restorative justice questions through teaching practices of conflict transformation and through research and engagement in issues of religious contributions to processes of transformative/restorative justice, especially in the U.S. prison system. She is an ordained elder in the Presbyterian Church (U.S.A.).

Miguel A. De La Torre is the Director of Iliff School of Theology's Justice and Peace Institute, Associate Professor for Social Ethics, and an ordained Southern Baptist minister. The focus of his academic pursuit has been social and political ethics within contemporary U.S. thought, specifically how religion affects race, class, and gender oppression. He has authored over fourteen books, including the award-winning *Doing Christian Ethics from the Margins* (2004); *Reading the Bible from the Margins* (2002); and *Santeria: The Beliefs and Rituals of a Growing Religion in America* (2004).

Gary Dorrien is the Reinhold Niebuhr Professor of Social Ethics at Union Theological Seminary and Professor of Religion at Columbia University. An Episcopal priest, he has authored thirteen books, including the three-volume *The Making of American Liberal Theology*.

Johnny B. Hill, a Progressive Baptist minister, is Assistant Professor of Theology at Louisville Presbyterian Theological Seminary. He is author of *The Theology of Martin Luther King Jr. and Desmond Mpilo Tutu* and has an abiding interest in the theology of reconciliation.

Elizabeth L. Hinson-Hasty is an ordained Minister of Word and Sacrament in the Presbyterian Church (U.S.A.) and Associate Professor of Theology at Bellarmine University. She is often called upon to speak in churches on issues concerning faith and public life. Her most recent books are *Prayers for the New Social Awakening,* co-edited with Christian Iosso, and *Beyond the Social Maze: Exploring Vida Dutton Scudder's Theological Ethics.*

Grace Y. Kao is an active member of Blacksburg Presbyterian Church (PC(USA)) and Assistant Professor of Religious Studies at Virginia Tech. Her work has appeared in the *Journal of the American Academy of Religion* and the *Journal of the Society of Christian Ethics,* among other places, and her first book is entitled *Grounding Human Rights in a Pluralist World: Between Minimalist and Maximalist Approaches.*

Rebecca Todd Peters is Associate Professor of Religious Studies at Elon University. She is an ordained Presbyterian Church (U.S.A.) minister and is currently serving as a member of the Faith and Order Commission of the World Council of Churches. She is the author of the award-winning *In Search of the Good Life: The Ethics of Globalization* and co-edited *Justice in the Making* and *Justice in a Global Economy: Strategies for Home, Community, and World.*

Marcia Y. Riggs is the J. Erskine Love Professor of Christian Ethics at Columbia Theological Seminary in Decatur, Georgia. Her books include: *Awake, Arise, and Act: A Womanist Call for Black Liberation* (1994); *Can I Get a Witness: Prophetic Religious Voices of African American Women* (1997); and *Plenty Good Room: Women versus Male Power in the Black Church* (2003).

Rosetta E. Ross is Associate Professor of Religion at Spelman College. She is an ordained elder in the United Methodist Church and has served on working groups for the denomination's General Board of Church and Society. Ross is author of *Witnessing and Testifying: Black Women, Religion, and Civil Rights* (2003) and co-author of the study *The Status of Racial and Ethnic Clergywomen in the United Methodist Church* (2005).

Darryl M. Trimiew is ordained in the Christian Church (Disciples of Christ) and the American Baptist Church and is currently the Chair of the Department of Philosophy and Religion at Medgar Evers College in Brooklyn, New York. His publications include *God Bless the Child That's Got Its Own: The Economic Rights Debate* and *Voices of the Silenced: The Responsible Self in a Marginalized Community.* Trimiew is the 2008 President of the Society of Christian Ethics.

Aana Marie Vigen is Assistant Professor of Ethics at Loyola University Chicago and an active lay member of the Evangelical Lutheran Church in America (ELCA). Her scholarly interests include topics such as healthcare inequalities, emerging medical technologies, ethnography in medical ethics, and notions of a "good death." Vigen is the author of *Women, Ethics, and Inequality in U.S. Healthcare: "To Count among the Living."*

Preface

Each era brings with it unique circumstances and responsibilities that challenge Christians to consider deeply what it means to be faithful in a time of crisis. The adversity, challenge, and change that are markers of human life mean that crisis is an intrinsic aspect of human life. Part of being human is figuring out how to respond to the world in which we live. Those with vision and passion will hopefully do more than simply respond, but will seek ways to transform the crises they face into opportunities for faith and growth and the possibility of a better world, and they will challenge others to do the same. This book is our response to the challenges that we have heard in recent years from our brothers and sisters who are living on the margins of society, in the United States and around the world.

Climate change, human trafficking, HIV/AIDS, health care, civil war, displaced persons, water shortages, poverty, and hunger are examples of a few of the crises that we face as a human community. Unfortunately, many of these crises have a disproportionate effect on people in the two-thirds world and people living in poverty in the first world. Not only that, but the wealth of the first world is often bought on the backs of the poor in many locales, and our consumer lifestyles translate into a disproportionate environmental impact compared with people in the two-thirds world. Concerned Christians in the United States and around the world are actively organizing to live out the gospel imperatives to "love our neighbor" and to care for the "least of these." As we listened to the voices of concerned Christians, three particular documents influenced the development of this book project.

The first two documents were recent statements made by the World Council of Churches (WCC) and the World Alliance of Reformed Churches (WARC) on globalization that have named the complicity of first-world Christians as part of the problem of neoliberal globalization in our world today. Primarily initiated by Christians in the developing world, the WCC's AGAPE document (Alternative Globalization Addressing Peoples and Earth) and the WARC's Accra Confession both challenge first-world Christians to study the issues and to respond as people of faith. These church statements make this book not only timely but also responsive to conversations in the global church. The AGAPE document and the Accra Confession provide alternative perspectives for first-world Christians to consider as we think about poverty, inequality, and environmental degradation in our world.

The third document is A Social Creed for the Twenty-first Century developed by the Presbyterian Church (U.S.A.) and the National Council of Churches to mark the one hundredth anniversary of the 1908 Social Creed that was part of the Social Gospel movement. A Social Creed for the Twenty-first Century is intended to promote dialogue in member churches and invite discussion about issues of social concern that face us as a nation and a global community. The 1908 and Twenty-first Century creeds focus primarily on economic injustice in the United States. Many issues raised in the latter creed are similar to those presented in the 1908 creed: the need for a living wage, the abolition of child labor, and the abatement of poverty. Other issues have changed since 1908. A Social Creed for the Twenty-first Century underscores the impact of globalization; includes mention of race, gender, and class in reference to economic, social, and political disparities; has a heightened awareness of the exploitation of our environment; and emphasizes the need to adopt simpler lifestyles for those who have enough. Social creeds represent a distinctive genre of writing that calls upon the larger church, local congregations, and members of churches to raise their own voices in a world that is all too familiar with injustice and violence.

The AGAPE document and the Accra Confession stand as the international background for considering domestic issues of social justice. As A Social Creed for the Twenty-first Century was revised and edited, responses to the document from scholars and activists from the Global South emphasized the importance of listening to the voices of those who had been most affected by the injustices named in the creed. In a global context, that means listening not only to U.S. American voices but beginning to make connections about how what we do affects others around the world. Our effort in this book to confront social injustice in the United States is informed by the good work that is being done by progressive Christians around the world. We invite others to call for more progressive public policies that will benefit those who are most vulnerable—socially, economically, and politically—in our nation. We also hope that U.S. Christians will begin to make the connections between what is happening in our domestic economy and what is happening more broadly in the global economy. As scholars, we see this book as a form of activism that we hope will invite conversation, discussion, and further action.

The authors for this volume are an intentionally diverse cadre of well-known, well-respected Christian social ethicists who are actively engaged with local and ecumenical church people and conversations. Each contributor adds a distinctive perspective through his or her own personal experiences and from his or her own justice-oriented work. We have had the good fortune as editors to work with contributors who were not only willing to labor in writing a chapter but also took the valuable time needed to meet as we formulated our ideas for the book. In May 2007, ten of the twelve contributors met at the Scarritt-Bennett Retreat Center in Nashville, Tennessee, to discuss the book and outline the individual chapters. All of the contributors were given copies of A Social Creed for the Twenty-first Century, the AGAPE document, and the Accra Confession as resource material for their chapters, which informed the development of the book. Through our discussions we identified the topics that needed to be addressed in individual chapters. The subjects of individual chapters correspond to issues raised by A Social Creed for the Twenty-first Century. We think that the collective wisdom gathered from the variety of perspectives represented in the book has made it a better and more useful resource. We also hope our process will not only enhance the quality of the book, but will also serve as a model for a dialogical process of engaging contemporary social issues in local churches. We see in this book both a challenge to the church to think more carefully about engagement in public life as well as a resource and guidebook for how to get involved.

Many other people and several organizations supported us in the process of our work. Our meeting would not have been possible without grants from Elon University and the Advisory Committee on Social Witness Policy of the Presbyterian Church (U.S.A.). We are very grateful for that financial assistance. Our editors at Westminster John Knox Press, Stephanie Egnotovich and Dan Braden, were immensely helpful throughout the process of editing the manuscript. We also gathered much strength from our families who gave us the support we needed to travel, tolerated our distraction as we edited the book, and served as dialogue partners as we formulated our ideas.

Elizabeth Hinson-Hasty
Rebecca Todd Peters

Introduction

Elizabeth Hinson-Hasty
and Rebecca Todd Peters

News of the ever-widening gap between the rich and the poor, escalating foreclosure rates, overly burdensome consumer debt, a public education system that too often leaves children behind, and the rising cost of health care cannot escape the attention of anyone in the United States today. Add to the list the swirling eddy of issues stemming from the war in Iraq, U.S. immigration policy, refugees unable to find a country to call home, and the human exploitation of our environment. These are but a few of the problems that leave people in the United States and around the world feeling overwhelmed. Lacking an abundance of simple solutions to our problems, we are in desperate need of people who will see the world and their role in it in a new way.

The purpose of this book is to offer a vision for public life and public policy in the United States that responds to the ways our economy marginalizes the needs of people and the earth. The chapters that follow explore how Christians have been and are currently engaged in social action. Our intention is to encourage you, as a Christian, to envision creative ways in which you can participate in social change in the twenty-first century. The authors, who are all Christian social ethicists and theologians, draw on deep and rich traditions of social justice and social activism that trace their roots back to the Hebrew prophets and the socially conscious and transformative ministry of Jesus of Nazareth. Jesus' life and work are a model for living faithfully in a world marked by sin, greed, and brokenness. Living as Christians in a pluralistic world requires that we work together with other people of faith and the larger community to address the social problems that hinder people from living lives of fullness and integrity.

In this book we articulate a vision for how churches can be engaged with public life in ways that help address social problems in our world. Along the way we share with you critical social analysis of these same problems. We ground our suggestions for action in a theology that challenges Christians to love their neighbors by addressing their concrete material needs and by transforming the structures in our society that prevent them from making ends meet and flourishing in the way that God hopes for all creation.

The term "progressive" has long been used to represent an understanding of Christianity marked by an awareness of social sin, a consciousness of institutional and human potential and shortcomings, and an emphasis on the church's mission to engage the world. While progressive Christians support charitable actions to meet the immediate needs of people in crisis, their deeper concern is to transform the social systems and economic structures of society that marginalize people and the natural world. Progressive Christians draw upon a variety of rich resources (Christian teachings and tradition, science, experience, social sciences, philosophy, etc.) to better understand society's problems so that we can work in collaboration with others to help our society, our world, and the church to move toward God's vision of a new earth.

Progressive Christians find firm footing for their social justice pursuits in Scripture. The concepts of covenant, hospitality, and justice lie at the heart of the biblical witness and fly in the face of the dominant social attitudes of power, responsibility, and individual freedom. Our common narrative as a faith community is rooted in the covenant relationship that God established with creation. This covenant tradition begins with Noah; is renewed with the descendants of Abraham, Sarah, and Hagar; and is renewed again by Moses on behalf of the Israelites. It implies not only a relationship between God and the people of God, but also that the people of God are a community bound together by bonds of kinship, faith, and responsibility. Through God's covenant the whole creation experiences God's blessing. The New Testament describes the actions of Jesus in the world as renewing the covenant between God and God's people to enjoy God's blessing, one in which the believing community is not only accountable to their kin and to God, but they are charged with offering hospitality to their neighbor. As Jesus interprets the Great Commandment "to love your neighbor as yourself" in the parable of the Good Samaritan in Luke 10, Jesus challenges his listeners to remember that their hospitality codes and obligations require the inclusion of strangers, enemies, and those who are in peril. In Matthew 25:34–40 he instructs his followers to feed the hungry, give drink to the thirsty, welcome the stranger, clothe the naked, care for the sick, and visit with prisoners. Jesus reminded others of their larger commitment to God's covenant relationship, a covenant requiring justice for the most vulnerable.

The witness of the Hebrew prophets in seeking social justice within their communities has offered guidance and wisdom to successive generations of Jewish and Christian followers. In the sixth chapter of Micah, God challenges the Hebrew people to remember how God acted to liberate them from the oppression of the Egyptians in the exodus. Micah challenges the Hebrew people to remember God's justice as the foundation of human action and asks, "What does the LORD require of you but to do justice, and to love kindness, and to walk humbly with your God?" (Mic. 6:8). In the Gospels, Jesus is remembered as standing within this larger Jewish prophetic tradition. Through his teachings and actions Jesus resisted the unjust laws of his time that served to marginalize and oppress. Luke challenges us with the memory of Jesus proclaiming, "The Spirit of the Lord is upon me . . . to bring good news to the poor, . . . release to the captives, . . . sight to the blind, to let the oppressed go free . . ." (Luke 4:18). These biblical values form the foundation for a progressive Christian worldview that can help Christians guide their behavior and actions as people of faith in the world.

A TRADITION OF SOCIAL ACTION

Churches in the United States have long responded to the biblical witness through social action. The abolitionist movement in the nineteenth century was, for many, rooted in religious beliefs and the conviction that the Bible laid out a case for the equality of the races. It was the duty of what abolitionist William Lloyd Garrison called "reasoning Christians" to speak out and work against social evils such as slavery and war, which were defended by Christians opposed to abolition. Further, Garrison argued, slavery meant bondage not only for slaves but also for the righteousness, order, and prosperity of all of American society. Former slave and abolitionist speaker Frederick Douglass criticized the slaveholders for using the church to "preach up the divine right of the slaveholders." Garrison, Douglass, and other abolitionists took great risks of their own to inspire many faithful people to confront unjust laws that kept the slaves in bondage. Other Christians, such as Levi and Catharine Coffin and Harriet Tubman, risked their own lives to assist slaves as they traveled to freedom on the Underground Railroad.

For many of the men and women who supported abolition—Susan B. Anthony, Antoinette Brown Blackwell, Douglass, Garrison, Sarah and Angelina Grimke, Lucretia Mott, Elizabeth Cady Stanton, and Sojourner Truth, among others—it became increasingly clear that the Bible also spoke of equality for women. The first Women's Rights Convention was held in 1848 in a Methodist church in Seneca Falls, New York. Antoinette Brown Blackwell gained a national reputation for her preaching and speaking on the causes of temperance, abolition, and women's rights. Breaking boundaries in church and society, Blackwell was ordained in 1853 by the Congregational Church, becoming the first ordained woman in the United States.

With the later nineteenth and early twentieth centuries came the Industrial Revolution and with it another set of social and economic problems specifically related to industrialization—child labor, poverty, and work conditions, to name a few—which drew the attention of people of faith. In response, the Social Gospel movement brought together committed Protestants to work toward much-needed social reforms in the United States and Britain. Social gospelers advocated for an eight-hour workday, financial security in old age and in the face of disability, the abolition of child labor, and the abatement of poverty. Social gospelers encouraged churches and church organizations to take public action. They published statements such as the Federal Council of Churches' 1908 Social Creed, which was revised over time as additional problems emerged. The 1908 Social Creed urged Christians to "uphold the dignity of labor" and to address issues such as a living wage, safety in the workplace, sweatshop labor, and provisions for adequate pensions. Social gospelers understood their actions on behalf of the most vulnerable in society as fulfilling the mission of the church. They questioned the churches' complacency in response to the social conditions of the working class. Walter Rauschenbusch, the most widely recognized Social Gospel theologian, alerted people of conscience to the stark contrast between God's vision for human well-being and the impact on the working class and other vulnerable people of the dominant economic policies and social practices. Rauschenbusch was optimistic that people could become more compassionate, increase their own consciousness of common human needs, and seriously make an impact upon the structures and systems that created poverty.

The optimism of the Social Gospel movement met with criticism from Reinhold Niebuhr, who, while taking social concerns seriously, also emphasized the reality of human sin and the limitations of human beings to address social problems. Niebuhr cautioned Americans not to become too self-assured and confident in their own government, even as the Cold War loomed during much of Niebuhr's lifetime. He became the church's public voice as he reminded Americans that any government, even our own democracy, has the potential to become a tool of oppression for others.

After Niebuhr, the church's public voice came through clearly in the voices of Civil Rights activists. Martin Luther King Jr.'s vision of beloved community echoed Rauschenbusch's emphasis on working toward a kingdom of God on earth but pushed Christians further so as to consider how race and class needed to be taken more seriously for real community to be lived. King's prophetic words and actions motivated thousands to act, to walk for miles, to stand in solidarity with the most vulnerable, and to change their lives in pursuit of greater promise. Women, such as activist Fannie Lou Hamer, also played key roles in garnering the energies of congregations. Hamer took personal risks as she registered voters, ran for Congress, and helped to create organizations that would address the living conditions of rural African Americans.

In the 1970s and 1980s, the involvement of Christian congregations in campaigns for peace led nearly every major denomination to call for a freeze on nuclear arms and to challenge the morality of nuclear war. Churches became involved in the Sanctuary Movement, offering asylum to Central American refugees fleeing human rights abuses and civil war. Their actions helped to bring the plight of Central American refugees to the attention of the American media. Christians traveled to Central America to accompany displaced communities, helped find transport for Salvadorans and Guatemalans to safer places in the United States, held ecumenical prayer vigils, protested human rights abuses, lobbied Congress, provided social services to refugees, sold Central American goods, bailed Central American detainees out of jail, and helped them file for political asylum.[1]

The economic recessions of the 1970s and 1980s led many Christian denominations to develop statements and actions of public witness addressing the economic inequalities of the nation and the plight of the poor. More recently, progressive churches have continued their concern for workers through their involvement in living wage campaigns, which are lobbying to secure fair and reasonable wages for the working poor, and in the Jubilee 2000 campaign, which is working to reduce the international debt of impoverished countries. Churches continue to take a leading role in calling for peace in a war-torn world. In January 2007, Christians concerned about unjust immigration laws and increasingly hostile deportation strategies joined together with Jews, Muslims, and Sikhs to launch the New Sanctuary Movement to protect undocumented workers and their families while working toward comprehensive immigration reform.

Progressive Christian movements have had a long-term impact in our society and the church. The abolitionists successfully humanized the conscience of many people and captured the attention of elected officials who could create laws that instigated change. Although it took seventy-two years from the first Women's Rights Convention until the Nineteenth Amendment was added to the Constitution, women did finally win the right to vote. Many of the reforms that the social gospelers advocated became part of President Franklin D. Roosevelt's New Deal: social security programs and federally defined fair labor standards are benefits still enjoyed by millions of Americans. No one can dismiss the power of the Civil Rights Movement that resulted in legal desegregation, increased voting rights for blacks, and the challenge of equality between the races that continues today.

The goal of progressive Christianity has been to ensure that people have access to the freedom spoken about in the Constitution and to hold our understanding of freedom accountable to the claims of justice rooted in Christian faith. When the Constitution originally protected the right of slaveholders and the slave trade, progressive Christians could not avoid Paul's statement that "in Christ there is no east or west, slave nor free." They saw themselves like the early Christian community in the book of Acts, which continued to teach and participate in acts of healing after Jesus' death so that "many signs and wonders were done among the people through the apostles" (Acts 5:12). Today we must draw upon this rich legacy and speak out clearly and loudly on social issues in hope of transforming the unjust systems in our world. The mission of the church in the public forum is to continue the work of healing, restoration, and reconciliation within God's creation.

A DISTINCTIVE WORLDVIEW

A worldview is the lens we use to understand and interpret the world and represents a set of ideas that shape how we see the world. Our worldviews are influenced by many things, including our religious beliefs, race, class, gender, education, and even the part of the country where we were raised. A progressive Christian worldview is distinct from others; it is rooted in three important principles that shape attitudes about the relationship between religion and politics and about what it means to be a Christian living in the United States today:

1. Christian faithfulness requires public action by churches and people of faith.
2. Christian social witness and public action should correspond to accepted practices of deliberative democracies.
3. The cause of social problems is often structural or systemic.

These three principles represent claims made by this book's authors about our world, human nature, the Divine, and our faith that help make sense of our problems as we seek solutions. As you read, you will see how these principles are rooted in Christian faith and tradition and how they offer a more comprehensive way of understanding and correcting social problems. Certainly a better understanding of our problems will help lead us to more effective solutions. We invite you to examine your own faith commitments and worldviews in light of these principles.

Called to Live Differently in the World

One goal of this book is to encourage you, as a Christian, to envision creative ways in which you and your community can participate in social change in the twenty-first century. We begin by inviting you to think about the first guiding principle:

Christian faithfulness requires public action on the part of the churches and people of faith.

Christianity is not simply a personal and private matter between an individual and God; it is also about community responsibility and faithfulness in public life—social, political, and economic. While this principle is neither new nor radical, it ought to guide behavior of individual Christians and Christian communities. The brief history of U.S. churches' engagement with social justice offered earlier in this chapter illustrates some of the ways Christians and their communities have embodied this principle.

Viewing our roles as Christians and citizens in holistic ways has the potential to offer more creativity and move us beyond simplistic solutions that do not adequately consider the complexity and interdependence of the world in which we live. As Christians living in a democracy, we have a special and unique opportunity to work together to confront the problems that are shaping social patterns and practices in destructive ways. Some may argue that the separation of church and state creates a deep line in the sand between matters of faith and matters of the world. However, it is unrealistic to expect people who have been shaped by the moral traditions of their faith to leave their religion at home when they enter the public square. Values often guide public decision making and the development of public policy, and whether those values are the values of the business community (profit and efficiency) or the values of religious communities (justice and care for the marginalized) can make a significant difference. Excluding faith from political debates bars an important resource for moral reasoning.

Moreover, the Constitution does not encourage Americans to keep our faith and our public life separate. What the First Amendment says is, "Congress shall make no law respecting an establishment of religion, or prohibiting the free exercise thereof," which means that there shall not be a single state religion, that all people of faith are free to practice their religion in this country, and that our government should not favor any one faith tradition. The separation of Christian life from public affairs creates an artificial boundary between the church and the state; it also makes an artificial boundary between our faith and the world. Christianity is not an individualistic faith; rather, Christians are called to live in community and to be active in the world in ways that witness to our faith in all areas of our lives.

The Role of Faith in Public Debate

As we live out our values and commitments in public as well as in private, we must also recognize the concerns many people have that as religion and politics interact, we run the risk of moving toward political and legal systems based on theological claims. Therefore, we must modify the first principle with this second one: Christian social witness and public action should correspond to accepted practices of deliberative democracies.

Deliberative democracies encourage decisions to be made by consensus and invest power in smaller groups working together to envision creative solutions for change. Leaving room for diversity of opinions, values, or contrasting worldviews to enter into the debate is a characteristic of deliberative democracy. This model allows for insights and perspectives rooted in faith experience to enter the public square. The variety of voices and perspectives also generates greater insight into the problems that we face and enables us to envision creative change as we engage in dialogue and work collaboratively with others.

Determining appropriate individual and public policy responses to social problems necessarily involves the discussion of values. These discussions can be difficult as we are confronted with ideas that are quite different from our own. A variety of factors in our lives—including families, communities, education, reason, and religious beliefs—shape our values. Because beliefs are, by nature, subjective and because different religious belief systems and values sometimes conflict with each other, relying upon exclusively religious justifications for social reform in the public forum, without attempting to find common ground with others, is not particularly effective, nor appropriate. While the Constitution protects our right as citizens to speak about faith in public discourse, it also protects the rights of those who do not share our faith claims.

The challenge then becomes *how* people of faith should bring their faith concerns and values to the table in ways that enhance and promote the common good. At the same time, in a religiously diverse community, we cannot expect our faith claims to have authority for people who do not share them. Therefore, as we move into public forums to debate and advocate for social change, it is important to identify commonly held values, ideals, or language that are consistent with our faith, but not exclusively derived from it. By identifying commonly held values, ideals, and language, we are able to facilitate a meaningful dialogue with people from different (or no) faith traditions as we work together toward change.

Martin Luther King Jr. provides an excellent model of combining the language of faith and the language of democracy to share his dream for a better world: "And when we allow freedom to ring, when we let it ring from every village and hamlet, from every state and city, we will be able to speed that day when all of God's children—black men and white men, Jews and Gentiles, Catholics and Protestants—will be able to join hands and to sing in the words of the old Negro spiritual, 'Free at last, free at last; thank God Almighty, we are free at last.'"[2] Christians are called to work collaboratively with others toward common public policy and social change goals, even if we do not share the exact same faith stories and motivations. Thus, while our faith motivates us to act in the world, we must develop language and moral arguments that allow us to debate with and enlist the support from those who may not share our faith commitments but do support democratic discourse in a pluralistic world.

Focusing on Structural Injustices

The third principle that underlies the essays in this book is the belief that social problems are not exclusively the fault of the individual but are often caused by structural or systemic failures. As we work toward developing public policy solutions to social problems such as poverty, racism, and crime, it is important to examine the structures and attitudes in society that support or exacerbate these problems. A structural or systemic analysis of social problems recognizes the power that is embedded in social structures and attempts to examine how lack of access to power and resources can negatively affect individuals whom those structures are supposed to serve. For example, while all children in the United States have access to public education, the quality of that experience varies widely—often along lines of race and class—in ways that further marginalize disadvantaged students.

Thinking about social injustice from a structural perspective requires refocusing the dominant worldview in the United States from its obsession with an individualism that views success or failure as the sole responsibility of the individual. While it is important to recognize and affirm individual human rights as vitally important to the health and well-being of our country, when individualism is taken too far, it is too easy to forget the common bonds of humanity that ought to bind us together into supportive communities and nations. Too much contemporary public policy grows out of a worldview rooted in an individualism that threatens to tear the fabric of our community apart. We all stand on the shoulders of others—our parents, teachers, ministers, mentors, friends, families, and all the other people who have contributed to our success and well-being in the world. Recognizing our interdependency is critical to effective social change. As we work toward developing public policy solutions to social problems such as poverty, racism, and crime, it is also important to examine how the structures in society contribute to or worsen these problems. Take, for example, current attitudes about poverty.

The most recent welfare reform legislation, the Personal Responsibility and Work Opportunity Reconciliation Act of 1996, was based on a worldview that assumed an individualistic cause of poverty—that poor people are lazy. This is not a statement of objective fact, but rather a claim that has been suggested as a guiding principle for understanding our world. Widespread popular acceptance of this claim limits our ability to understand poverty, which can have a significant impact on public policy. One of the assumptions underlying this legislation was that if poor people simply learned how to be more responsible, then they would not be poor anymore. But legislation based on the assumption that the poor are lazy is unable to attend to the multiple sources of oppression that confront people living in poverty—low-wage jobs; inadequate or no health care; disability; depression; domestic violence; sick children; lack of affordable, high-quality child care;

physical and mental illness; and inadequate education. If we examine the U.S. Census data, we discover that in 2005 there were 37 million people living below the poverty line in the United States. Thirteen million of those living in poverty are children. Furthermore, 60 pecent of those families had at least one working family member.

Some Christians justify the existence of poverty by using Jesus' own words, "You always have the poor with you" (John 12:8), as a theological excuse to allow poverty to persist and to emphasize the culpability of individuals for their own impoverishment. It is difficult to reconcile that interpretation with Jesus' other words and actions. Jesus was more likely reminding his audience of the teachings of the Torah: "There will, however, be no one in need among you . . . if only you will obey the LORD your God by diligently observing this entire commandment that I command you today" (Deut. 15:4–5).

Because significant causes of social problems lie in society's institutions and structures—our education system, our tax policies, the criminal justice system, the military, the banking system, the healthcare system, to name a few—the approach to studying those social problems must be both more nuanced and more thorough, and must include an examination of long-term strategies of resistance and healing. Each of our lives is touched by these structures in a variety of ways throughout our lifetime. Some of us benefit from these systems by procuring a solid education, by obtaining a loan to buy a car or a house, through safe streets or communities, or a safe and healthy childbirth. These same systems fail others through, for example, inadequate schools, lack of access to health care, and racial discrimination in lending.

Our intention in this book is not to condemn these structures, but rather to compare how they are intended to function in society with how they actually function. Social problems can rarely be pinned down to a failure in any one system, but are often the result of several contributing failures that send a person into poverty, prison, or worse. We invite you to look more closely at the ways in which many of the problems in our country are rooted in an unjust social order that continues to discriminate along lines etched by race, class, gender, and nationality. Statistics show that disparities in health care, education, the housing market, poverty, the criminal justice system, wages, and employment are correlated to race, class, and gender. Too often, people confuse correlation with causation. To understand the *causes* of these social disparities, it is necessary to examine the underlying structures of injustice in our society. Understanding any one social problem in our society in isolation is impossible. Problems in the criminal justice system are related to problems in the education system, which are connected to problems with employment and housing. While each of the chapters addresses a single issue, we hope you will notice how often these topics and problems overlap and interconnect.

CONCLUSION

As progressive Christians committed to moving the level of moral discourse in our nation beyond personal morality and overly simplistic solutions to complex problems, we do not offer here a single, universal proposal for change; to be honest, no single solution is possible. The essays that follow explore the social dilemmas we are most concerned about today: difficulties faced by families, unfair treatment of undocumented workers, increased militarization, the exploitation of the earth, poverty-level wages and their impact upon workers, the importance of social safety-net programs like Social Security, tax policies that favor the common good, the quality of public education, affordable housing, the impact of current drug policy, the adequacy of our criminal justice system, and lack of access to adequate healthcare. These problems and proposals to create change will be explained and discussed in light of Scripture, tradition, science, and lived experience. Our aim is to challenge common assumptions and to prompt new ways of thinking about what makes sense in and for our world. We also highlight the creative ways that progressive Christian communities have and can address the problems we are facing. Our goal is to propose and invite further discussion about a social agenda that has the potential to create healthier, more egalitarian, relational, and inclusive practices in our society and Christian communities. To that end, we include questions for reflection and additional resources for your use.

A majority of people in the world claim to be religious. Communities of faith around the world possess the potential to address the social problems that currently plague our country and our world. However, the transformation of hearts, minds, and communities that is required to accomplish this task is deep and profound. This transformation must come from within individuals and communities. We sincerely hope that thoughtful, faithful Christians around the country who are willing to seriously engage in this conversation will discover that they, in fact, share our progressive belief in structural analysis and social change as foundational to Christian life. We also believe and have hope that the world can be something different than it is today. God is calling us to work toward reconciliation and healing in everything that we do. We hope that fruitful discussion will also lead to action and that progressive churches will think of creative ways to more fully and faithfully attend to the problems described in the chapters that follow. The world will only change when people work to change it. Progressive Christian communities represent a powerful partner in the work to abolish poverty, reform our education and criminal justice systems, redress racism and ethnocentrism in our communities, and transform the United States into a peaceful and responsible global ally.

NOTES

1. Susan Bibler Coutin, *The Culture of Protest: Religious Activism and the U.S. Sanctuary Movement* (Boulder, CO: Westview Press, 1993), 3.
2. Martin Luther King Jr., "I Have a Dream," in *A Testament of Hope*, ed. James M. Washington (San Francisco: HarperSanFrancisco, 1986), 220.

Chapter 1

For Workers

ELIZABETH HINSON-HASTY

A story has been told about advice that Clarence Jordan, Baptist minister and founder of Koinonia Farms, gave to a pastor who complained that he could not persuade the board of deacons at his church to increase the custodian's pay. Jordan asked the pastor how many children the custodian had to support. The pastor replied, "Eight." Jordan then inquired as to how many children the pastor had. "Four," the pastor responded. Knowing that the pastor made more money than the custodian, Jordan suggested that the pastor "swap salaries" with the custodian and thought the problem was solved.

I have heard this story used as a sermon illustration that raised not only significant questions among members of the congregation but also some anger. For some, it seemed unnatural to pay the custodian, whose job was considered to be less prestigious, the same amount as, if not more than, the pastor. Others wondered why the pastor who preached this sermon did not "practice what he preached." The preacher's congregation at the time paid its custodial staff minimum wage. The point that seemed obvious to Jordan was that remuneration for work should not be set according to what job society considered more prestigious or by value judgments placed on what was considered "good" or "bad" work. Pay should not even be set according to the value placed upon it by market competition. If we believe that all human beings are valued by God and created as equals in God's image, then wages should reflect the value of workers by covering workers' basic needs.

The practice of considering the needs of others along with one's own individual and family needs is firmly rooted in biblical teachings and a long Christian tradition. The author of Acts characterized the early Christian community in this way:

> Now the whole group of those who believed were of one heart and soul, and no one claimed private ownership of any possessions, but everything they owned was held in common. . . . There was not a needy person among them, for as many as owned lands or houses sold them and brought the proceeds of what was sold. They laid it at the apostles' feet, and it was distributed to each as any had need. (Acts 4:32, 34–35)

What might we as a society and in Christian community gain by practicing an ethic that considers the needs and interests of others along with our own self-interest? How would we need to reconsider the economic value placed upon different forms of work in American society? What changes would need to be made for our society and our Christian communities to reflect the ideal that there would not be a needy person among us—where all can satisfy their own basic needs?

LOW-WAGE WORKERS: THE NEEDY AMONG US TODAY

Individuals who earn the current federal minimum wage of $5.85 an hour and work full-time for fifty-two weeks a year will only earn $12,168 before taxes. This will barely raise them above the 2007 federal poverty guidelines of $10,210 for a single person and is nowhere near enough to support a family. The current federal minimum wage is set to increase incrementally to only $7.25 an hour by 2009. Think for a moment about how much $47.00 (the present minimum wage times eight hours a day) a day can buy where you live in the United States. Would it be enough to afford a decent place to live? Adequate food? A reliable car? Necessary trips to the doctor? What if you were also supporting dependents and had to pay for day care, clothe your children, or buy prescriptions to alleviate chronic illness? The vast majority of minimum-wage workers also lack important benefits such as retirement and health insurance.

Many people assume that the average minimum-wage worker is a teenager working at the local McDonald's and living at home with his or her parents. Others think that people working minimum-wage or low-wage jobs are unskilled and deserve low pay because of some fault of their own. Statistics show, however, that the average minimum-wage worker is an adult woman, over twenty years old, who has earned at least a high school diploma and has family responsibilities. Minimum-wage workers earn the lowest wage that employers are allowed to pay workers as established by federal law. According to the Economic Policy Institute (EPI), 79 percent of minimum-wage workers are adults and 59 percent are women. The majority of minimum-wage workers are white women. EPI estimates that 13 million workers (10 percent of the workforce) currently will be affected by the increase in the federal minimum wage that goes into effect in 2009.

In addition, a larger proportion of African American and Hispanic workers earn poverty-level wages than white workers. A poverty-level wage is defined as an hourly wage which if worked full-time and year-round does not total enough to meet the federal poverty standard for a family of four. For 2005, the federal poverty-level wage was $9.60 an hour. EPI found in its study *The State of Working America 2006/2007* that 29 percent of women workers and 20 percent of male workers earn a poverty-level wage. Thirty-seven percent of black women and 29 percent of black men, and 35 percent of Hispanic men and 46 percent of Hispanic women earn a poverty-level wage. Another category of workers are the more than 30 million Americans, about one-quarter of the American workforce, who work low-wage jobs. Low-wage households bring in more than the minimum wage, typically earning two times the federal poverty standard. In 2007, the federal poverty guideline was defined for forty-eight states, excluding Hawaii and Alaska, as $20,650 for a family of four. The percentage of African American and Hispanic workers affected by low wages is far higher than their overall representation in the workforce.

Many think that fast-food restaurants employ the highest percentage of low-wage workers. In reality, fast-food jobs make up only a small percentage of low-paying jobs. Other low-wage jobs include the people whom we depend upon most to be skilled caregivers, such as day-care providers, home health aides, and nurses' assistants. Security personnel, food service workers and processors, cooks, maids, cashiers and pharmacy assistants, agricultural workers, and laundry and dry cleaning employees also fall into the low-wage category.

These statistics became real to me when I took a class to the Salvation Army Center for Hope in Louisville, Kentucky, and met Lydia. Our assignment was to break bread with the homeless and other impoverished people dining at the center. In conversations around our tables, we learned that several of the people who were homeless worked full- or part-time. I ate dinner with Lydia and her two children. Lydia worked full-time in a Laundromat, washing and folding clothes for customers paying by the pound for their laundry to be done. Although she and her children lived in low-rent temporary housing provided by the Salvation Army and ate dinner at the shelter most nights, she expressed her optimism about her own future: "Things are gonna get better. I just need to get more education and get some benefits." Lydia shares a belief held by many

Americans. If she works hard enough and gets enough education, then she will be able to "pull herself up by her bootstraps" and lift herself out of poverty.

Unfortunately, recent trends do not support such optimism. Political agendas often focus on education as the means to create economic upward mobility for people who are poor. Today, the majority of low-wage workers have earned a high school diploma. Some have even earned a college degree. In the past, education may have helped workers gain entrance into the middle class but upward mobility is becoming increasingly difficult even for those with some education. The Bureau of Labor Statistics reported in 2005 that between 2004 and 2014 the greatest growth in employment will be in the "service-providing sector," often the lowest-paying occupations and which do not require college degrees.

The circumstance of low-wage jobs generates a great deal of instability in workers' lives. Low-wage jobs are more likely to require working nonstandard, more rigid, and less stable hours. Unpredictable work schedules make it more difficult for a worker to plan for child care, get an education, and keep in contact with extended family and organizations that provide networks for support. Unstable income causes more frequent changes in residence, including the increased likelihood of eviction, being forced to live without utilities, and, for children, more absences from school. Low-income workers are at a disadvantage when trying to establish consumer credit, making it difficult to afford reliable transportation. When credit is approved it is often at high interest rates. Many live without phone or Internet service and opt to live with others or rent rooms in budget-rate motels. Workers paid low wages have greater difficulty affording nutritious foods. Government subsidies for crops such as corn, wheat, and rice make carbohydrate-heavy foods cheaper than healthier fruits and vegetables. Statistics show that about 38 percent of low-wage workers receive health insurance from their employers, compared to 69 percent of higher-wage workers. Individuals and families without health insurance lack access to consistent medical care, and medical care is often simply unaffordable for low-income families. In times of illness the only available medical care may be the emergency room, which is extremely expensive.

These examples bring to life patterns that are becoming norms for workers. Beth Shulman, author of *The Betrayal of Work,* invites us to reconsider assumptions made about the responsibility placed upon individuals for their poverty. The accumulation of wealth of the people at the top of the employment ladder is linked to the poverty experienced by those at the bottom. Shulman argues that "the great secret of America is that a vast new impoverished population has grown up in our midst. Yet these are not Americans who have been excluded from the world of work; in fact, they make up the core of much of the new economy. Indeed, our recent prosperity rests, in part, on their misery. Their poverty is not incidental to their role as workers, but derives directly from it."[1]

Paying low wages allows businesses and corporations to offer low consumer prices and enjoy high stock prices, while putting billions of dollars of profits in the pockets of investors, CEOs, and other executives.

"APARTHEID ECONOMY"

Harvard economist Richard Freeman writes that

> income inequality in the United States has massively increased. This jump owes to the unprecedented abysmal earnings of low-paid Americans, income stagnation covering about 80 percent of all families, and an increase in upper-end incomes. The rise in inequality—greater than in most other developed countries—has reversed the equalization in income and wealth we experienced between 1945 and 1970. The United States has now cemented its traditional position as the leader in inequality among advanced countries.[2]

Freeman argues that these inequalities have the potential to create an "apartheid economy," in which the lives of working-class and poor people are fundamentally and qualitatively different from those of middle- and upper-class people.

Traditionally, economists have argued that wages are based upon market competition and that employers themselves have little or no power to set wages. Many owners of businesses, both small and large, will also claim that they simply cannot afford to pay higher wages. Deviating from the wage being paid by their competitors could mean that they will sustain losses and be forced out of the market. Therefore, the market itself sets limits upon workers' wages through competition. However, no such limits are placed upon the salaries of corporate executives. According to Forbes.com, the highest-paid CEO in 2006 was Apple executive Steve Jobs, who hauled in $647 million in vested restricted stock. Forbes.com also reported that in the same year CEOs of America's five hundred biggest companies received an average pay raise of 38 percent. Economist James Galbraith challenges a traditional approach to understanding the determination of wages. He argues that we need "a rebellion against the idea that people are actually paid in proportion to the value of what they produce . . . We need a rebellion, not so much against existing market institutions, *as against the analytical tyranny of the idea of the market,* as it applies to pay."[3]

Reduced government regulation gives major corporations tremendous power to shape American social and industrial policy. Economists, journalists, and academics lift up Wal-Mart as an example. Nelson Lichtenstein, professor of history at the University of California, Santa Barbara, observes that Wal-Mart's revenues outreach those of the entire country of Switzerland. As the largest employer in twenty-five states, Wal-Mart has tremendous economic clout to set the domestic standard concerning wages and benefits for many other corporations.[4]

People have varied reactions to critiques of Wal-Mart because they enjoy and benefit from cheap goods. In some areas, particularly rural areas, Wal-Mart may be the only option for shopping within several miles. For many poor people, it is also the only place that they can afford to shop. Wal-Mart is appealing to many Americans because it promotes itself as a patriotic corporation whose practices are rooted in Judeo-Christian values and the Protestant work ethic. Lichtenstein interviewed several Wal-Mart workers who commented that they appreciated the friendly atmosphere where employees remained on a first-name basis with their managers. But Wal-Mart is no friend of laborers at home or abroad.

Wal-Mart and many other discount retailers depend upon cheap labor to amass their profits. The discount king employs 7.5 million workers around the world, winning it the title of the largest private employer in Mexico, Canada, and the United States. Wal-Mart considers thirty-two hours a week full-time employment (eight hours less than full-time as defined in 1938 by the Fair Labor Standards Act).[5] Contrast the wages of hourly workers at home and abroad to that of Wal-Mart CEO H. Lee Scott who, according to Forbes.com, earned $60 million this decade at an average of $8.5 million a year. Journalists Peter Goodman and Philip Pan reported that Wal-Mart encourages Chinese factories to cut costs in order to supply cheaper goods. In a Chinese factory the journalists visited in 2004, workers were paid only about $120 per month in American dollars without benefits.[6] The average Wal-Mart worker in the United States is paid $8.23 an hour (a poverty-level wage).

Wal-Mart opposes unions, leaving workers little or no negotiating power with the corporation, but even unionized workers employed by other companies are having a difficult time fighting these trends. Unions were once strong and enjoyed stronger support from the U.S. government. In the first half of the twentieth century, unions helped people fight for better wages, an eight-hour workday, and security in old age and sickness. Our government has done much in the last thirty years to limit the bargaining power of unions.

It would be unfair to cite corporations as the only organizations allowing tremendous disparities in pay between workers and upper-level management. Churches sometimes take cues from the market when establishing compensation packages for their staff. In my presbytery, the Presbytery of Mid-Kentucky, the salary in 2006 for the highest-paid pastor was more than ninety thousand dollars a year (not including benefits), twice as much as the associate pastor on staff at the same church. Some congregations in the same presbytery are unable to pay a full-time pastor. In the Presbyterian Church (U.S.A.), minimum standards are determined for the compensation of pastors, but no minimum standards are set for the fair compensation of Christian educators, church secretaries, or custodians. The result is an accepted order for pay in churches that fails to consider the needs of all those called to serve the congregation.

ARE COMPASSIONATE CAPITALISM AND CHARITY ENOUGH?

The response of many economists, business leaders, and religious people is that these problems can be solved by nurturing greater compassion in the marketplace and by more effectively utilizing the work of charitable organizations. But is compassionate capitalism coupled with charity enough to address the issues people in poverty are facing?

Business leaders and economists advocating for a more compassionate capitalism think that, as a philosophy and system, capitalism is not inherently bad. They point to the tremendous economic growth that a free market has created. Economist Deirdre McCloskey argues in her book *The Bourgeois Virtues* that, by appealing to and nurturing compassion within individuals, capitalism as a system can and actually is improving its moral record.[7] Business leaders should be more virtuous and treat workers with fairness. What we must do is fully embrace capitalism so that jobs will be created and the market itself will establish fair prices and fair wages. McClosky, however, does not seem to take into account the fact that CEOs and other leaders cannot exercise compassion without losing their own share in the market. Can we simply rely on the good nature of individuals to be more benevolent in their treatment of workers? Don't we need more governmental regulation as well as individual transformation?

So many people fall through the market's cracks. Charity has been seen as another way of responding to the needs of people living in poverty. While charitable organizations have done good and important work to address the needs of many of the working poor, charity does not transform systems that cause workers to live in poverty. Charitable programs are designed to address crisis situations. The majority of social ministries focus on programs that alleviate the economic stress placed upon many families by providing emergency assistance but fail to pay attention to the systemic causes of people's poverty. The Immokalee workers provide a good example.

Primarily Latino, Haitian, and Mayan farmworkers, the Immokalee workers pick tomatoes in Florida that are later supplied to Yum! Brands, the corporation that owns Kentucky Fried Chicken, Taco Bell, Long John Silvers, and Pizza Hut. Although the farmworkers worked full-time they were not paid enough to support themselves. Many relied on charitable organizations when money fell short. Noelle Damico, United Church of Christ pastor and director for the Campaign for Fair Food for the Presbyterian Church (U.S.A.), has observed that charity relieved the strain in crisis situations, but had the effect of subsidizing the businesses that were unwilling to pay workers adequately for their work. Giving financial aid to businesses is a form of corporate welfare that enables businesses to earn profits from lower labor costs but leaves workers vulnerable. Fortunately, the Immokalee workers led a successful boycott of Yum!

Brands that was supported by a variety of churches and the wider public. Yum! committed itself to paying just a penny more per pound for tomatoes, and the workers' wages increased significantly.

The living conditions of poor people and the economic disparities that we see along the lines of race and gender are causes for moral outrage. A more compassionate capitalism coupled with the charitable work of religious organizations may help but will not adequately attend to the problems before us. Neither compassionate capitalism nor charitable programs adequately address the systemic nature of these problems. Our economic policies and practices must be changed so that people who work are valued and the needs of individuals and their families along with the larger community are kept in mind.

Do you remember the parable of the Workers in the Vineyard found in the Gospel of Matthew? In the parable, Jesus compares the kingdom of heaven to a landowner who goes out to hire workers for his vineyard. The landowner goes to the marketplace five different times during the day from early in the morning to late in the afternoon. On each trip to the market he finds workers and sends them to work in his fields. With the first group of workers the landowner agrees to pay them "whatever is right." Late in the afternoon, the landowner expresses concern that there are still workers in the market who have been unable to find a good day's work. Even at such a late hour he sends them to his fields to work. At the end of the day the workers gather for their pay and the landowner pays them all equally. Of course the workers grumble. Some had labored in the fields from early in the morning. The landowner replies:

> "Friend, I am doing you no wrong; did you not agree with me for the usual daily wage? Take what belongs to you and go; I choose to give to this last the same as I give to you. Am I not allowed to do what I choose with what belongs to me? Or are you envious because I am generous?" (Matt. 20:13–15)

This story offers us great challenge because it flies in the face of the competitive spirit we have been conditioned to accept. Jesus' parable invites us to consider the idea that the greatest value should be placed upon the *people* who work, above values for work determined by the marketplace.

MORE THAN JUST THE MINIMUM: CREATIVE WORK FOR CHANGE

There are good examples of businesses and Christian communities who are doing much to value workers and to practice an ethic of generosity. Seven years ago Malden Mills, manufacturer of Polartec and Polarfleece fabrics, was destroyed by fire. Rather than moving the mill overseas, CEO Aaron Feuerstein rebuilt in the same location in Massachusetts and paid his workers as the mill was being rebuilt. A devout Jew, Feuerstein commented to reporters that "I have a responsibility to the worker both blue-collar and white-collar. . . . I have an equal responsibility to the community."[8] COSTCO offers another good example. It is often assumed that businesses, especially discounters, simply cannot afford to pay fair wages. However, COSTCO, a discount retailer, pays workers an average of seventeen dollars an hour with benefits. Sol Price, the owner of COSTCO, rejects the notion that discounters can only profit by giving their employees short shrift.

Some Christians, like those at Koinonia Farms, distance themselves from dominant social and economic structures to witness to a different way of life. Other Christian communities participate in our shared economic structures and push them from within. Religious communities and labor unions have worked together to advance living wage laws across the country. The idea behind the living wage is that full-time workers will be paid enough so that they won't have to depend upon government assistance programs such as Medicaid and food stamps. In the late 1980s, Madison Avenue Presbyterian Church cooperated with other church-supported groups, religious people working in soup kitchens and homeless shelters, workers, and union organizers to form a coalition that backed a living wage campaign in Baltimore. The city had poured thousands of dollars into urban renewal by giving tax incentives to businesses, but the businesses primarily created low-wage jobs. Together, their coalition applied pressure on the local governance until in December 1994 Kurt Schmoke, mayor of Baltimore at that time, agreed to sign the Social Compact that they had proposed. The Social Compact included raising the minimum wage to $6.10 an hour with an increase over time to $7.70 an hour and recognizing the workers' negotiating organization, the Solidarity Committee.[9]

We have so much to gain by attending to the social and economic structures that are creating an ever-widening divide between rich and poor. The call to Christians today is to challenge assumptions that place the burden of the responsibility for poverty upon the shoulders of individuals alone. We must confront the notion that the market itself has the ability to fairly determine wages and cannot be changed. We should challenge tremendous economic disparities between the salaries of those at the top of the company ladder and those at the bottom. Our call is to speak the truth about policies that will ensure that all workers are paid enough so that they can satisfy their own basic needs as well as the needs of their families. Policies should be changed even when it means that we have to take economic risks of our own and transform the systems that have created such inequalities. Workers should be valued not only because of what they contribute to our common life through their work but because they are valued by God.

The prophet Isaiah speaks about God's vision for a world where God's people will not "build and another inhabit; they shall not plant and another eat; for like the days of a tree shall the days of my people be, and my chosen shall long enjoy the work of their hands. They shall not labor in vain . . ." (Isa. 65:22–23). I cannot help but think that this is God's vision for all people today.

QUESTIONS FOR DISCUSSION

1. Investigate the cost of living in your area. What would be a "living wage"? How can and should workers and employers go about determining how much is enough to be self-sufficient? How have religious communities in your area been involved in advocating for adequate wages for all workers?
2. Do you think there are moral limits to profits for individuals and corporations? If so, how much should corporate executives be allowed to make? Two times the salary of the lowest-paid worker? Five times? Ten times? Twenty? Where do you think our society should draw the line so that the needs of all workers are met?
3. Some churches establish minimum salaries for their pastors. Do you think that churches should establish minimum salaries for all of their staff, including custodians, administrative assistants, and Christian educators? Do you think churches should establish maximum salaries for their pastors?
4. What do you think that we as a society and in Christian communities have to gain by considering the needs of others along with our own individual needs? What do you think we have to gain by ensuring that all people who work are paid enough to satisfy their own basic needs?

RESOURCES

Books

Harper, Nile. *Urban Churches, Vital Signs: Beyond Charity toward Justice*. Grand Rapids: Wm. B. Eerdmans Publishing Co., 1999.

Shulman, Beth. *The Betrayal of Work: How Low-Wage Jobs Fail 30 Million Americans.* New York: New Press, 2003.

Sklar, Holly, and Paul H. Sherry. *A Just Minimum Wage: Good for Workers, Business and Our Future*. With a foreword by James A. Forbes Jr. Philadelphia: American Friends Service Committee, National Council of Churches USA, 2005.

Web Sites

The Economic Policy Institute: Research for Broadly Shared Prosperity, www.epi.org.

Let Justice Roll: Faith and Community Voices Against Poverty, www.letjustice roll.org.

Living Wage Resource Center, www.livingwagecampaign.org.

NOTES

1. Beth Shulman, *The Betrayal of Work: How Low Wage Jobs Fail 30 Million Americans*. New York: The New Press, 2003, 4.
2. Richard B. Freeman, "Solving the New Inequality," *Boston Review*, December 1996/January 1997, http://bostonreview.net/BR21.6/freeman.html.
3. James Galbraith, *Created Unequal* (Chicago: University of Chicago Press, 2000), 266.
4. Nelson Lichtenstein, "Wal-Mart: A Template for Twenty-First-Century Capitalism," in *Wal-Mart: The Face of Twenty-First-Century Capitalism,* ed. Nelson Lichtenstein (New York: New Press, 2006), 4.
5. Ibid., 27.
6. Peter S. Goodman and Philip P. Pan, "Chinese Workers Pay for Wal-Mart's Low Prices: Retailer Squeezes Its Asian Supplier to Cut Costs," *Washington Post,* February 8, 2004, A1.
7. Deirdre McCloskey, *The Bourgeois Virtues* (Chicago: University of Chicago Press, 2006), 22–33.
8. Avi Shafron, "Aaron Feuerstein: Bankrupt and Wealthy," http://www.aish.com/societyWork/work/Aaron_Feuerstein_Bankrupt_and_Wealthy.asp.
9. Nile Harper, *Urban Churches, Vital Signs: Beyond Charity toward Justice* (Grand Rapids: Wm. B. Eerdmans Publishing Co., 1999).

Chapter 2

For Families

GLORIA H. ALBRECHT

What do we want for our families? A crowded table with enough food to satisfy the hunger of several generations gathered together? Time to share memories and tell stories? A place called "home" where one is known intimately and loved fully? The comfort of knowing that there are people in one's life who will be there through thick and thin, agreements and disagreements, joys and sorrows? What do we expect of families? That they provide loving care, pass on wisdom, teach values, practice virtues, and shape moral character for the building up of neighborhood and community? Aren't these our ideals?

Families are, after all, our first school of justice. No social institution has yet taken the place of families for providing the human need to be loved and valued or in forming moral character through the daily, small, repetitive practices that shape a way of seeing and living life: sharing income, stretching food and clothes to meet the needs of each, giving care, feeling compassion, treating each person with equal respect. In the family, children experience their first example of adult relationships. Are they manipulative? Dominating? Cooperative? Egalitarian? They have their primary experience of others more and less powerful than themselves. How is power used? Families perform the meaning of gender daily and pass it on to a new generation. Is it equal or unequal? Rigid or fluid? Families open and close doors to others. Who is welcome? Who excluded? Who is "we" and who is "they"? These lessons become embedded in our sense of self. We carry them into future relationships and live them out as citizens. What families do, and how they do it, is critical to the understanding of justice, fairness, and human rights that we take into our society.

Jonathan Kozol describes his conversation with Cliffie, a seven-year-old living in the poorest congressional district in the United States. His mother sent him to the store once to get three slices of pizza: one for each parent and one for Cliffie. But on the way back he saw a homeless man, freezing and hungry. The man pointed at Cliffie's pizza.

"What did you do?" asked Kozol. "I gave him some," answered Cliffie. "Were your parents mad at you?" Cliffie looked surprised at this question. "Why would they be mad?" he asked. "God told us, 'Share!'"[1]

It is also true, however, that family life is shaped by the larger social and economic context. When the possibilities for individuals are limited by racism, sexism, heterosexism, or economic injustice, families suffer and adapt to survive as best they can. The personal is really also political and economic. Families will produce the kind of people prized by the values of the political economy. As progressive Christians, we reflect on what public and economic policies embody the biblical concept of the covenant community: a community characterized by members entrusting themselves to an enduring and faithful relationship, even in the face of a member's betrayal. As Ruth said to Naomi, "Where you go, I will go; where you lodge, I will lodge; your people shall be my people, and your God my God" (Ruth 1:16). Such is God's covenant with us. Created in God's image and blessed by God with life and dignity, humans are called by God to act together as God's stewards, assuring that God's blessings, given freely to all, are enjoyed by all families. Blessed by God's covenantal promise of faithfulness to us, Christians accept God's call to be faithful in our responsibility to others for the quality of our common life together. We know that as we shape human affairs we can bring forth, or thwart, the well-being God intends for all. We affirm that values like commitment, responsibility, and concern for others are important personal values essential to good families; they are also important social values, characteristic of the covenant community we are called to be and to create.

Asthma is the most common disease among children in Cliffie's neighborhood. Cliffie has asthma, too. The asthma mortality rate in this black and Hispanic neighborhood is nine times more than in the virtually all-white neighborhood of Staten Island. Kozol describes the lack of preventive care, the cost of inhalers and other medications, the prevalence of noncertified "doctors" in streetfront clinics, and long waits in hospitals.[2]

WHOSE FAMILIES COUNT?

As we rethink how to share God's blessings with the families of the earth, we need to consider what a family is. Most of the institutions of our society, and most of our church practices, assume one form of "family": two married heterosexual parents with children and a husband as primary (or sole) breadwinner. Tax policies, Social Security benefits, school schedules, bosses' expectations, church dinners, hospital visitation policies, health insurance, and pensions—you name it—all assume this "normal" family. Conservative Christians would say that this is the way it should be: public policy should reward the "right" form of family. Don Eberly's statement is typical, "Whatever else the debate is about, it must be primarily and predominately about shoring up and rebuilding the intact two-parent family. Everything else is secondary."[3] In the name of the one right form of family, conservatives have opposed a variety of social policies that seem to aid and abet what they consider to be inferior and dysfunctional families: cash assistance to poor single mothers, tax-supported child care, civil unions and marriage rights for same-sex couples, paid family leave, domestic partner benefits, and so forth.

Yet, in our churches and neighborhoods and families, past and present, many other forms of family exist. Look at your relatives, your neighborhood, your church, and your own family history. What other forms of family strive with courage, love, and hopefulness to do well what families do best: nurture children, care for dependent adults, share resources, sustain intimate bonds, and pass on values and traditions? Because they do this, we call them "families." They may have one, two, or no biological parents in the home. Members may not share the same residence even as they take responsibility for one another. They may be adults without children. They may have different or same-sex partners. They may have no partner. The meaning of "family" has always been plural, to capture the differing stages of life and life's unforeseen events. Today, it must also capture the differences in human sexual orientation. The well-being of all families, not just married families, is a covenantal concern that cannot be reduced to "heterosexual" or "married."

ARE FAMILIES UNDER ATTACK?

Almost everyone agrees that U.S. families are in trouble. It is a topic of hot debate. One view often passed off as "common sense" on talk radio and in socially conservative circles says the problem is personal values. Just look at the divorce rate, the unmarried birth rate, the danger to marriage from same-sex couples, and the poor's lack of commitment to hard work. From this point of view, the crisis facing families is rooted in "me-first-ism": the prioritizing of individual gratification. The solution is marriage and its disciplines, 1950s style. As they say on talk radio, lifelong heterosexual marriage will solve poverty, drug addiction, high school dropout rates, teen pregnancy, and most other social ills.

How true is this oft-told tale? Family life has certainly changed since the mid-twentieth century. The percentage of first marriages ending in divorce has gone from 25 percent in the 1950s to around 43 percent today. The percentage of families headed by single mothers has increased substantially: from 12 percent of all families with children in 1970 to 26 percent of such families in 2000. While the teen birth rate has been falling since the 1950s, the rate of nonmarried teen births doubled to its current rate by 1990. The percent of family households that are married with children has declined from 40 percent of all families in 1970 to 24 percent in 2000. Families with same-sex partners, unmentionable in the 1950s, are now counted in the census: about 1.6 percent of U.S. families. More than 30 percent of these families have one or more children.

As the story gets told, good family life has gone out of style and in its place are bogus substitutes, like single-mother and same-sex families. How ideal was that 1950s ideal? How "traditional"? Why did these changes happen? What were their social origins? Are they bad? We need some historical perspective.

Let's start with the divorce rate, which actually began to rise in the 1890s. By 1946, 33 percent of marriages ended in divorce. In this long-term upward trend, the lower rate of the 1950s is the anomaly—not the norm. Moreover, the upward trend leveled off in the 1980s. With better health and longer lives, couples today are more likely to celebrate their fortieth anniversary than were couples one hundred years ago! This is no dismissal of the seriousness of divorce, but it is a recognition that, in the past, marriage was very rarely a fifty-year project. Death intervened. Today, longer lives, greater opportunities for women, and respect for the sexual orientation of persons are positive social changes. But they, and the changing economic context discussed below, bring different expectations to marriage, family, and gender relationships.

If we turn to teenage birth rates, we find they were twice as high in the 1950s as they are today. But pregnancy in the 1950s led to teenage marriage, and the age of first marriage fell to a one-hundred-year low. The consequences of dropping out of high school were different at that time. Fifty years ago, white males had a pretty good chance of getting entry-level jobs that led to a middle-income standard of living. The wages of low-income workers were rising faster than the wages at the top. Good jobs were created as the federal government poured money into public works: water and sewer systems, highways, and school construction. And lots of (mostly white) families benefited from the G.I. Bill that made getting a college education and buying a new house in the new suburbs possible at the same time. In an expanding economy with strong unions, the wealth created by workers' productivity was shared more broadly. Corporations and the wealthy paid much higher taxes while most (white) families could achieve a middle-income living standard with the wages of only a husband.

Sound good? It was—for many. But there is also a dark side to the 1950s. It was a time of harsh and pervasive discrimination against women, racial/ethnic men, non-Christians, and gays. Women, marrying younger, became mothers younger and lost educational ground to men. Victims of child abuse, domestic violence, and violence aimed at sexual "deviants" had no recourse, no shelters to which to escape. Twenty-seven percent of the nation's children lived in poverty; almost 50 percent of African American married-couple families were poor. Few black soldiers returning from the war received any G.I. benefits. And the term "race riot" meant angry, armed white folk attacking black families and torching black neighborhoods. Detroit alone recorded hundreds of such incidents in the 1950s and 1960s.

If we are going to be nostalgic about 1950s families, I would point to the liberal political economy of the era that supported them—that is, if we could strip it of its racism, sexism, and heterosexism. Generous government programs, a growing economy, rising wages for average- and low-wage workers, and stable employment were the conditions that created the broad (white) middle class of U.S. society. The changes in our political economy since then, from "liberal" to "neoliberal," do not get much air time on talk radio. It's easier to tell people to "get a job" than to acknowledge the growing economic burdens on most families, the unleashing of destructive forces in the global search for more profit, and the slashing of government programs that once represented some commitment to shared blessings.

GLOBALIZATION AND GROWING ECONOMIC BURDENS FOR FAMILIES

In the United States today, having a job is essential to the well-being of most families. The existence, location, and working conditions of jobs, however, are based on strategies designed to increase profits of business owners or investors. Sometimes these interests clash. In 1996, Phillips–Van Heusen announced that it would be closing three of its U.S. factories. One was the factory in Clayton, Alabama. Phillips' CEO said this closure was necessary to save the jobs of their other U.S. workers. In 2006, Phillips closed its manufacturing plant in Ozark, Alabama—its last plant in the U.S. In 2007, the company reported a 17 percent gain in revenues and projected a total gain of 15 percent over 2006. Analysts gave the stock a "buy" rating. Today, in Clayton, Alabama, the median household income is $24,352. Thirty percent of its families live below the poverty line, including 38 percent of its families with children and 58 percent of its single-mother families. Phillips now buys its clothing products from factories in Jordan, Honduras, Guatemala, and Saipan, where it has been cited for labor violations.

Poverty anywhere is not a family value, yet the United States has the highest overall poverty rate (17 percent) and the highest child poverty rate (21.9 percent) of all advanced countries. About 25 percent of U.S. workers earn poverty-level wages, including 33 percent of African American and 39 percent of Hispanic workers. Those who do caregiving work for pay, disproportionately women of color, are some of the lowest-paid workers in the workforce. Researchers tell us that poverty is the most common factor in teen pregnancy, and that economic stress is one reason for the higher rate of divorce among lower-income families.

Yet economic stress is expanding as the old employment contract of the 1950s disappears. Since the 1970s, the wages of most nonsupervisory U.S. workers (70 percent of the workforce) have lost real value. Fewer employees are covered by health insurance plans even as worker contributions and deductibles have increased. Less than half of the workforce is covered by employer-provided pension plans, and most of those are defined contribution plans (like 401(k)s) that depend on workers' successful investing. The impact of each of these antifamily practices is felt more harshly by Hispanic and African American workers. For example, only 29 percent of Hispanic workers were covered by employer-provided pension plans in 2000 compared to 55 percent of white workers. Still, we continue to read grim stories of downsizing, layoffs, givebacks, offshoring, and restructuring. In June 2007, many papers carried this story: "Workers at the bankrupt Delphi Corporation approved an agreement today that would eliminate a long-time job security protection program and steeply cut their hourly pay. . . . [Delphi] demanded steep wage cuts in a bid to become more competitive. . . ."[4]

Families adopt survival strategies as society loses its covenantal commitment to family well-being. They work more hours; the average U.S. worker works more hours a year than workers in any other rich industrial nation. They add another worker to the workforce; the additional income earned by wives and mothers since the 1970s kept low-income couples from losing ground altogether and helped middle-income couples make some gains. Today, women make up almost half of the U.S. workforce and most work full-time. Most mothers of young children are also employed. When mothers choose to work part-time to balance their family responsibilities, they experience a lower hourly wage for doing the same work, no benefits, and little chance of promotion. Due to racial disparities in wages and benefits, black and Hispanic families put in many more hours of work to achieve the same income level as white families. Is it any wonder that single-mother families, regardless of race (but not single-father families), have a high rate of poverty: 36 percent?

As the workplace becomes less "family-friendly," family responsibilities intensify. You may have heard of work-family stress. You, like Jean in the following anecdote, may be living in it. Jean works in a food-processing plant in a U.S. town:

> When I started, the time was 7 a.m. It was understood when I started that my children go to the daycare from 6:30 a.m. until 5:30 p.m., so that I could not possibly come in earlier than seven and stay past five. . . . Anyway, they changed the starting time to 6 a.m. and we have to stay until we

> are finished, even if it's after 5 p.m. You stay or you are terminated. . . . My neighbor is going to take the . . . kids at 5:30 in the morning so I can get to work at 6. That means we'll be getting up at 4:30. . . . The company really didn't give me any choice.[5]

If the values of a society can be determined by where it puts its time and money, then the outlook for our families is bleak indeed. Neoliberalism, with its mantra of "small government," celebrates the reduction of government funding for programs that support families and that could even lift families out of poverty. With its mantra of "free trade," neoliberalism celebrates the globalization of the labor market, the weakening of labor unions, the erosion of the real value of the minimum wage, and every reduction in the cost of labor. We have seen the benefits of economic growth and worker productivity being siphoned from most U.S. families into the hands of the few. In the neoliberal global economy, families must bear the increasing burdens as a society rejects its covenant commitments. But some families, especially low-income families, single mothers, and disproportionately families of color, are faced with truly tragic choices: take care of your children or lose your job; work overtime or lose your job; take a pay cut or lose your job; leave the oldest in charge of the youngest or lose your job; work a different shift than your spouse/partner so that your children are not alone or lose your job.

BUILDING THE COVENANT COMMUNITY

What would it mean for our political economy to value families? Families need adequate time and adequate income to do the work of families upon which the well-being of society depends. A political economy that denies these basic goods to families, whether in the name of "family values" or in the name of "free trade," or, in some parts of the world, "development" and "progress," destroys the basis of human well-being. It not only threatens the physical well-being of our families, but their moral quality as well. It is not only a matter of physical poverty, but of spiritual poverty, too. Threatened by social forces they cannot control, families rich, poor, and in-between hunker down into a "me-first-ism" that shrivels their ability to care about others. Threatened by a harsh and unjust political economy, they take adaptive reactions, not all of which will be successful.

The call to Christians is to restore the covenant nature of community; to shape economic and public policies for sharing God's blessings adequately and fairly among all. Policies that move in that direction are already in place in other advanced countries: mandated paid leave for the care of children or other dependents; mandated flextime and paid vacation time; tax-funded child-care systems and universal healthcare coverage; transfer payments and other programs for low-income families that are generous enough to lift many families out of poverty. We can make part-time work good work, and we can get living-wage legislation passed in our towns. We can open ourselves to new possibilities by recognizing that the purpose of any political economy is to serve the needs of community by promoting human flourishing-in-community. We can begin to change our own consciousness by valuing equally, if not more, the work of families as well as the work of production. We can insist that workers be treated as the parents, caregivers, spouses, partners, and friends that they are, and we can begin to do this in our own churches and wherever we exercise employment power. We can learn how social policies work that support families in other nations, and we can challenge our government to do as well. We can find out what the needs of families are in our neighborhood, our church, and our church's neighborhood—and we can strategize to get those needs met. We can do all this in the confidence that God has covenanted to walk with us and to work through us to heal our brokenness.

QUESTIONS FOR DISCUSSION

1. For one week, keep a record of the types of families you encounter. Through personal conversations or through organizations representing a family type, find out what stresses different family types have in common, and which are different. Begin a list of what can be done to support families of different forms in your church, your community. What can you or your congregation work on?
2. How have neoliberal policies impacted families in your church and community? Have jobs been lost? Gained? Are wages higher than a decade ago? Lower? What is a "self-sufficiency" wage for your community? What percentage of the community has health insurance coverage? A pension plan? What percentage of your community lives in poverty? What differences in economic well-being do you discover between races and genders?
3. Do your family practices model the form and content of justice that you envision for your society? Do the normal practices of your church model an inclusive justice? Why? Why not? What can the workplace and the church do to support your family's values?
4. What organizations in your community work for worker justice (domestic and global), the alleviation of poverty, or the enrichment of egalitarian family life? What can you and your church learn from them? How can you support their work?

RESOURCES

Books

Albrecht, Gloria. *Hitting Home: Feminist Ethics, Women's Work, and the Betrayal of "Family Values."* New York: Continuum, 2002.

Heymann, Jody. *Forgotten Families: Ending the Growing Crisis Confronting Children and Working Parents in the Global Economy*. Oxford: Oxford University Press, 2006.
Nelson-Pallmeyer, Jack. *Families Valued: Parenting and Politics for the Good of All Children*. Friendship Press, 1996.
Schein, Virginia E. *Working from the Margins: Voices of Mothers in Poverty*. Ithaca, NY: Cornell University Press, 1995.

Web Sites

Children's Defense Fund, http://www.childrensdefense.org.
Human Rights Campaign, http://www.hrc.org.
Interfaith Worker Justice, http://www.iwj.org.

NOTES

1. Jonathan Kozol, *Amazing Grace: The Lives of Children and the Conscience of a Nation* (New York: Crown Publishers, 1995), 8.
2. Ibid., 170–72.
3. Don Eberly of the National Fatherhood Initiative, quoted in William Raspberry, "Superfluous Father Syndrome," *Washington Post*, March 9, 1994.
4. *International Herald Tribune*, June 29, 2007.
5. Virginia E. Schein, *Working from the Margins: Voices of Mothers in Poverty* (Ithaca, NY: Cornell University Press, 1995), 49.

Chapter 3

For Those Affected by Drugs

DARRYL M. TRIMIEW

As I gazed over the forty thousand hectares of barren land, I realized that I was in a state of shock. I was in Putumayo, a southern region of Colombia, actually the coca tree–growing capital of that nation. Looking over the denuded field, barren as far as the eye could see, I had difficulty understanding how so much land could be left bare, given the poverty that I had observed in the region. Besides being shocked, I was also angry, because I had also just seen thirty thousand hectares of recently planted coca trees. What game was being played here and who were the players? Why was I in this Alice in Wonderland situation?

My presence there was no game or fantasy. I was there as a delegate for Witness for Peace, a Christian not-for-profit organization that was trying to stop the oppression of *campesinos*, or "peasants" in Colombia. We had flown to Putumayo from the capital of Colombia, from Bogotá, to see what was going on in the countryside, an area being torn apart by a longstanding civil war.

The farmers who had planted the new acres of coca plants were poor peasants, people of the land who had families and bills and who survived on subsistence living. They also had their pride and a firm belief in God. Interestingly enough they believed in the same God as I do, Jesus Christ. As Witness for Peace delegates, in

Bogotá, we had previously met with a wide range of Colombians. Some were quite wealthy—cattle barons, oil magnates, and industrialists—with large estates and servants. Some were simply citizens, urbanites just trying to make a living and striving to rear their children. Others were the absolutely displaced, marginalized people of that country, the Afro-Colombians who had been forcibly removed from their land up north.

To me, Colombians were a friendly and generous people. In meeting people from all walks of life, we did, of course, get a variety of opinions on the coca production and trade. Why were there denuded fields?

As all of the representatives in Colombia shared with us, the U.S. government had given the Colombian government millions to spray Round-up, a popular powerful herbicide, to kill coca plants. As part of its billion-dollar "Plan Colombia," our government has facilitated spraying Round-up from airplanes in its so-called war on narco-terrorists.

The army general whom we met in Putumayo was proud that he had been educated at the infamous School of the Americas, or S.O.A., an American training school associated with developing the mastery of arrest, detention, and torture techniques of dissidents. Charming and soft-spoken, he explained carefully his important mission of fighting communists and narco-terrorists on behalf of his country. From his perspective, peasants growing coca were simply accomplices to drug trafficking. He was fully in favor of the ongoing program of deforestation that the American government was financing.

I might have been moved by and admired the general's words had I not already visited an indigenous village and seen young children and infants with open running sores caused by eating contaminated banana, yucca, and corn from sprayed fields. The awful reality in Putumayo is that *campesinos* plant coca alongside all of their own conventional crops. If you spray one crop from the air, you spray them all. This known fact did not disturb the army or the cattle barons or the oil magnates we had met in Bogotá. They did not get their vegetables and fruit from sprayed fields.

Up and down the roads in Putumayo, oil pipelines connected little villages like La Hormiga (the Ant) to other hamlets. This area has, of course, more than just peasants, coca, and bananas; it also has oil. Oil exploration of the area was not complete, and unsurprisingly, many of the peasants farmed land that oil explorers wanted to explore. Naturally, if peasants were to abandon their family's ancestral plots, exploration could be conducted in a much easier and more complete fashion. So spraying continued. The poverty and suffering did also.

"Why do you continue to plant coca?" we asked the peasants.

"We must," they said, "in order to pay for our children's shoes and education." In a poor agricultural society, every dollar counts.

"Don't you know that this product is refined and shipped overseas and poisons millions?"

"No," they replied. "All we know is that coca is easy to grow, easy to transport to market." Coca need not be fresh, clean, or palatable to sell; bananas, corn, and yucca require much more care. "We do not use the coca, and we do not know what goes on in the U.S. with the leaves. We only know that we must struggle and work hard in order to survive here."

As I heard that last reference to survival, over and over again, from a wide variety of peasants, I reflected back on my practice of criminal law in the late 1970s and early 1980s. "Why do you persist in selling crack when you know that it is illegal, that you can get killed in the trade and at best, will probably get locked up if you do not quit?" I had asked some of my clients, charged with drug violations. Many of my clients, pooled-out defendants from the public defender's office, would listen to my question impatiently and then reply, "We must sell this shit in order to survive here. We have families to feed and rent to pay and no other work in sight."

In the United States, with great fanfare, our newspapers constantly trumpet the latest big arrest and prosecution of drug traffickers, and yet drug trafficking persists at relatively the same levels, year in and year out. "Man is born free, but everywhere he is in chains," Jean-Jacques Rousseau said, and the truth of his observation is quite evident when we look at our current state of national drug addiction. From the jungles and fields of Putumayo, Colombia, to the hard urban streets of Newark, New Jersey, my hometown, trafficking in cocaine in one form or another appears to be a necessity for some of the marginalized people of both societies.

"What else can we do?" asked the *campesinos*. "When we tried to raise fish in the farm pond projects that the government encouraged, the government still sprayed over our farm ponds and killed all of our fish!"

"With nothing to bring to market I must plant coca where and when I can."

"What else can I do?" asked many of my clients in Newark. "With our broke-down education, jobs moved out of the city, and no prospects in sight, how else can I survive?"

I was faced with the real problems of people on the edge. These people were not playing games. Growing up in Newark, New Jersey, before the 1967 and 1968 riots, I was the beneficiary of an excellent public school education, even though my school was located in a drug-infested community. I remember classmates getting high in the bathrooms in junior high school. While drugs were a plague in Newark, even at that time, people still had blue-collar jobs in the city, and Newark had a working-class population, and a white-collar middle-class one also. People still shopped in downtown Newark. Suburban malls and suburban sprawl were on the horizon, but not yet on the scene. In a transient state of economic viability, drug trafficking was present but it was not, at that time, the only game in town. Perhaps if interdiction (the practice of vigorous arrest, trial, conviction, and sentencing) had been more vigorously pursued then, it could have been effective in halting drugs. Even as late as my law school years (1972–75) I was still a true believer in drug interdiction and a staunch opponent of the decriminalization of "hard drugs." It was not yet apparent (at least not to me) that more stringent law enforcement could neither minimize nor eliminate the problem. Like most Americans, I was scandalized when the mayor of Baltimore, Maryland, Kurt Schmoke, called for the decriminalization of drugs. Interdiction was, I believed, the key, the right public policy. My theology, morals, and legal opinions were prescriptive rather than descriptive. Doing drugs was wrong, and therefore interdiction must be right. I held firmly to this conviction until I found out the truth in Putumayo and elsewhere. At that time, I did not ask the most appropriate ethically responsible question, "What is going on?" It is only after that question is asked that other questions can be addressed. The truth of our circumstances comes out of rigorous examination of prevailing conditions.

What is the truth about the drug trade? The undeniable truth is that the illegal drug trade is a multibillion-dollar industry, yet at the beginning point of production in the cocaine trade, the growing of the coca trees in Colombia, the growers are poor. Moreover, at the end of the chain in Newark, New Jersey, and elsewhere, most of the "clockers" or street pushers are also poor. Some of them a little higher on the American end of the trade might grab a brief fortune to finance their bling. Nevertheless, most of them crash and burn eventually, as they are sentenced to federal prisons for long and unproductive incarcerations. As a seminary professor in Fort Worth, Texas, I frequently took some of my classes to the federal penitentiary. There we found that 70 percent of the inmates were incarcerated due to drug-related crimes: that was what was going on. Most of the inmates worked in the sign shop, making highway signs and license plates for the state of Texas. This trade would not be available to them should they serve out their sentences and wish to get legitimate work after being released.

Roger Betsworth, a noted Christian ethicist, has written, "To be human is to be self-deceived." With this observation he is only echoing the Bible. Jeremiah 17:9 reads as follows: "The heart is devious above all else; it is perverse—who can understand it?" Frequently, our human condition dooms us to playing games, and the person we most frequently deceive in this process is ourselves. We continue to support international interdiction even though we now have decades of poor results showing that the cocaine trade, for example, is spreading to other countries rather than being curtailed. Coca trees are now being planted in the Amazon rain forest where they have never been previously planted. This practice is also exacerbating the destruction of invaluable rain forest. Albert Einstein once famously observed, "One is insane, when one keeps on doing what one has been doing but continues to expect different results." After years of failed drug policy, we need not be Einsteins to realize that the continued ineffectual practice of interdiction cannot yield the results that we desire, namely, the minimalization of the practice of drug trafficking and drug addiction.

At first glance, the argument for decriminalization can certainly seem immoral. Surely the use of drugs should be a crime, and therefore it must also be a sin. Why should any Christians and churches, progressive or otherwise, champion the proliferation of sin? This question deserves a careful response.

The question should, however, be stood on its head. Because the use of drugs is addictive and enmeshes people in a practice of sin, alienating them from God and from everyone around them, the use of drugs should be minimized for the good of all. This form of public policy thus lends itself best, in terms of moral analysis, to a consequentialist approach. In a world of sin, drug addiction, like many sins, cannot apparently be eliminated. It should, nevertheless, at least, be minimized. Thus, two progressive practical questions should be, What regulatory steps can be taken to minimize the use of drugs? And what regulatory practices should be taken to minimize the international criminal enterprise of drug trafficking? These are good questions that are seldom posed with regard to our current practice of ineffectual interdiction. In order to answer them intelligently, they should be addressed in reverse order.

If what we most want to accomplish with reference to public policy is to minimize the international drug trafficking enterprise, interdiction is clearly the wrong approach. Why? A quick review of Prohibition explains it. Carrie Nation, a Disciples of Christ woman of faith, led, along with many others, a war against alcohol that resulted in the passage of federal legislation that ushered in the era of Prohibition. The moral motives of the teetotalers were impeccable; they wished to eliminate "demon rum" and thereby create a "good society" that was more sober, fit, and dependent upon God for help, comfort, and recreation. While the motives were admirable, the results were abominable. Not only did people continue to drink alcohol, an admittedly dangerous drug if abused, but its sale was removed from legal vendors and exploited by illegal vendors, manufacturers, and distributors. Suddenly, from coast to coast and across international borders, gangsters were in their own little Wonderland. Now they had sole control over a commodity that legitimate businesses could not sell, a large and age-old market demanding a continued supply of a product, and willing accomplices everywhere: namely our historic bootleggers and white lightning distillers who, like our *campesinos* and clockers, were themselves frequently located in economically marginal communities. My memory flashes back to my own grandfather, who as a poor black mechanic in Richmond, Virginia, also ran a still, up north, in Hanover County, Virginia. Suddenly, during Prohibition, common hoods had the opportunity to exploit such a large and lucrative illegal trade that organized crime was fully capitalized rather than undercapitalized. It quickly became more capable of committing more crimes, more violence, and did so with more money than it had been able to acquire previously through more traditional crimes and vices such as gambling, prostitution, and loan-sharking. A common inexpensive spirit such as whiskey or beer overnight had an artificial surplus of value. Furthermore, this surplus value was not returned to still operators in Virginia, Kentucky, and elsewhere. Like clockers and *campesinos*, still operators (like my paternal grandfather) just made a living. Organized crime, however, made a killing. Suddenly there was surplus value by which to bribe judges, police, and money launderers and to turn thereby otherwise morally weak and vulnerable people into felons. And here is where our comparison finally hits home. If in our current predicament clockers and *campesinos* are not winding up with the enormous profits, who is collecting the filthy lucre? As in the days of Prohibition, the financial beneficiaries of the international drug trade are high-level dealers and money launderers. Why should they, the most morally corrupt players in this game, continue to be supported by bad public policy? How do they contribute anything good to the commonweal? How can they ever be expected to help to minimize the sale or use of drugs? They cannot, for it is their livelihood and they need to profit from sin and crime.

Who will save us from this body of death? Jesus is our Lord, but Jesus is neither responsible nor in charge of public policy; we the American people are. If the artificial surplus value of drugs was removed from the drugs, much like it was for alcohol with the repeal of Prohibition, then that surplus value would not be available to organized crime: this is the aim of decriminalization. If cocaine, for instance, was dispensed at governmentally regulated centers, where users were compelled by law to register, then whatever surplus value was generated by the trade would be available to the government for use for counseling, education, addiction treatment, prevention, and even more rigorous interdiction of high-level dealers. If our government controlled the distribution of extremely dangerous drugs, we would know where the drug users are and where their drugs came from, and they, the addicts, would have a chance to receive the treatment they need to kick their habit. In a worse-case scenario, addicts would continue to kill themselves by continuing to do drugs, as many are doing currently in an America that has no national health care access to readily available drug treatment centers. This result is tragic, but again, this essay assumes that sin cannot be eliminated by human beings, but only by God. Public policy can, in contrast, minimize social, economic, political, and cultural practices that encourage, facilitate, and continue the proliferation of suffering, crime, and sin.

Furthermore, if we now turn, finally, to our second question, we find that it has been addressed by our first question, which was: what regulatory steps can be taken to minimize the use of drugs? If we change public policy from ineffectual interdiction to intelligent decriminalization, admittedly we will not be eliminating drug addiction directly. But as Prohibition has taught us, government and public policy cannot eliminate well-established vices. We can, however, promote the avoidance of drug use in the same way that we now, more effectively, curtail the use of tobacco. In particular, revenue generated by government-regulated drug manufacturing and distribution can fund school programs that educate our children about the hell of drug addiction. If we really care more about actually preventing the beginning of addiction, especially the addiction of our children, by providing timely and effective drug prevention education, are we not more morally wise in doing so, rather than merely sneering at and punishing our addicts? Of course if we do provide appropriate preventative education, perhaps we will not need to build more prisons, hire more police, and incarcerate more people. Perhaps our prison industrial complex, our burglar alarm systems industry, and the need for additional taxes to pay for more police would decline. In our admittedly imperfect world, with fewer addicts needing to commit fewer crimes to pay for their drugs, we might all be more secure. Of additional moral consideration is the possible improvement of our moral landscape with reference to the middle-management players whom we have not examined carefully. What has been going on with them?

In order to facilitate the flourishing of the international drug trade, bankers, police, bail bondsmen, and the judiciary must be bribed. Drug lords have no qualms in providing the bribes, which are the grease necessary for the wheels of the criminal enterprise to keep spinning. Once bribed, our public servants become the drug lords' private slaves. This additional sin and crime cannot be curtailed or even minimized by continued interdiction. As some crooked police and judges are ferreted out, prosecuted, and punished, others (like the previously mentioned clockers and *campesinos*) simply take their places. None of these public servants—the police, bail bonders, or judiciary—are exceptionally well-paid. If the bribes are sufficiently high (and because of the artificial surplus value of illegal drugs, they can be) some, in every generation, are bound to succumb eventually. In other words, we have created a situation in which the advantages of vice are maximized and the advantages of virtue are minimized. In moral analysis this situation is one of moral minimization and immoral maximization, which by any measure of analysis is morally wrong.

Yet can a government engage in decriminalization without furthering drug use and making a bad problem worse? The truth and reality are that other governments have already done so and their efforts have helped to minimize the worse depredations of the drug trade.

In Western Europe, Denmark and Holland, among other countries, have decriminalized some drugs. In so doing they have regulated governmental distribution of drugs and achieved lower rates of drug use, incarceration, recidivism, and drug-related crime than has been possible in America. In other words the policy of minimizing the worse aspects of the drug trade has already been implemented successfully. Why then are we in the United States still carrying as a burden on our backs the wrong approach to minimizing the drug trade? Our current policy of interdiction allows us to claim, without compromise, that we are opposed to the drug trade. Such claims may make us feel good about ourselves, and such healthy self-regard has a value. Our zero-tolerance policy affirms our puritanical tradition of staunchly resisting any concessions to sin. Such a policy may make those of us who are not addicted and who do not live in drug-infested areas feel superior to those of us who are not so fortunate. As a personal virtue, a lifelong commitment to sobriety and abstinence is a social good and should be nurtured and encouraged. Our churches, schools, and most importantly, our homes should facilitate our efforts to live lives of such virtue. As a private policy we have a duty to keep our bodies as unpolluted temples provided by God and available for use solely for God's purposes. This is a Christian virtue and duty. Yet as Christian actors in the public sphere, our personal commitment to holiness and abstinence should not prevent us from endorsing and implementing public policy that minimizes the flourishing of the drug trade. In other words we would not be sending mixed messages in consistently teaching, in our churches and other institutions, that drug use should be avoided at all costs, while supporting the decriminalization of hard drugs so as to minimize drug trafficking and use for those who have not been able to achieve or maintain lives of abstinence.

Another way of looking at this situation is to try to understand the drug trade as an illegal business that facilitates the exploitation of "sick" people for its profit margins. Drug addiction understood as a disease does not, theologically speaking, divorce it conceptually from the notion of drug addiction as also an expression of sin. It is a sin and a disease in the same way alcoholism is. Indeed, the decriminalization of hard drugs is a stricter and more stringent response to that problem than is our present policy with regard to alcohol use and alcoholism. Currently we merely restrict the purchase and use of alcohol to adults and forbid sales only to children. *Decriminalization is not legalization.* Decriminalization would not permit the distribution of drugs without governmental regulation, registration, counseling, and oversight. Here is the choice: we can continue with our demonstratedly ineffectual public policy of interdiction without decriminalization, whose primary benefit is to make us individually feel good about ourselves (we, the nonaddicted, that is). Or alternatively, We can confess, with more humility and honesty, that we all fall short of the glory of God. We can admit that a public policy change that may not perfectly coincide with our personal values but would greatly help others who are failing to overcome their addictions is in fact the morally superior response. Indeed, decriminalization does not even compromise my personal rejection of drugs since in no way does it incline me or anyone else to use drugs. It does not entice me to sin, nor does it erase my troubling memories of Putumayo, Rahway Prison, or the mean streets of Newark, New Jersey.

Nothing can erase my last memory of my grammar school friend Paul. Paul was an excellent student. Paul was kind and considerate and quiet and my main academic rival. The last time I saw Paul, however, was on my first trip home from college in 1969. Emaciated and glassy-eyed, he could barely stand up (a victim of heroin addiction). He was obviously near death. I saw him on the street and was stunned by his horrific change. I merely greeted him and walked away. That next week I read his obituary in the paper. Paul failed in our society, but our society also failed him. We can, like Pontius Pilate, wash our hands and walk away from the Pauls of our communities. We can close our eyes to the clockers on the streets, or the emaciated and sick children of Putumayo. We can merely enjoin our police to produce more law and order, like Romans who wanted their legions to produce more Pax Romana. Or instead we can say that we, as Christians, that we the Church, can push for public policies that discourage the proliferation of fates like Paul's. Jesus Christ claimed, in Luke 4:18, that he came to preach good news to the poor and came to set the captives free. We cannot be sinless like Christ, but we can institute public policy that helps the addicted to set themselves free. We can facilitate drug education that prevents, however imperfectly, further addiction. We can proclaim good news to the poor, and in doing so we can stop playing games and instead compassionately intervene in the sad games people play. We can help create a better world, or we can continue to play games. What would Jesus do?

QUESTIONS FOR DISCUSSION

1. The current approach to eliminating illegal drug trafficking is interdiction (the practice of vigorous arrest, trial, conviction, and sentencing). What are the main reasons to consider the decriminalization of drugs? Do you think the decriminalization of drugs can be an appropriate Christian response to the drug problem in this country? Why or why not?
2. How are drugs and drug trafficking affecting your community? How can you and/or your congregation get involved in addressing the significant problems of drug trafficking and drug addiction in our country? What are short-term solutions? What are long-term solutions? What obstacles do we face and how might Christian communities overcome those obstacles?
3. Trimiew discusses drug addiction as both disease and sin. What does he mean by "sin" in this context? Do you agree or disagree? Why?
4. In the case of drug trafficking and drug addiction does the end justify the means if decriminalizing drugs has the effect of lowering drug use and reducing crime and incarceration? Do you think that Christians would send mixed messages by consistently teaching that drug use should be avoided at all costs while supporting decriminalization of drugs?

RESOURCES

Coombs, Robert H., and Douglas Ziedonis, eds. *Handbook on Drug Abuse Prevention: A Comprehensive Strategy to Prevent the Abuse of Alcohol and Other Drugs*. Upper Saddle River, NJ: Prentice Hall, 1995.

Driver, Tom F. "Colombia's War." *Christian Century,* November 7, 2001, 14–17, 19.

Husak, Douglas N. *Legalize This! The Case for Decriminalizing Drugs*. London: Verso Publishers, 2002.

Joyce, Elizabeth. "New Drugs, New Responses: Lessons from Europe." *Current History,* Philadelphia: April 1998. Vol. 97, Is. 618; 183.

Myers, Steven Lee. "Army Training School to Rise Again, Recast but Unmoved." *New York Times,* May 20, 2000.

Thomas, Charles, "Promoting Peaceful Alternatives to the War on Drugs," http://idpi.us/dpr/dpr_writings_offdrugs.htm.

Wink, Walter, "Getting Off Drugs: The Legalization Option," http://idpi.us/dpr/writings/writings_offdrugs.htm.

Web Sites

Interfaith Drug Policy Initiative, http://www.idpi.us.
Witness for Peace, http://www.witnessforpeace.org.
Drug Policy Research Center, http://www.rand.org/multi/dprc.
Schaffer Library of Drug Policy, http://www.druglibrary.org/schaffer/index.htm.
School of the Americas Watch, www.soaw.org.

Chapter 4

For Prisoners and Our Communities

ELIZABETH M. BOUNDS

I can name quite clearly the times in my life when the injustice in front of my eyes has overwhelmed me to the point of nausea. There was the time, for example, when I visited Nanjido, the city dump for Seoul,[1] and saw the houses perched on the side of mountains of garbage, while their inhabitants, covered in dirt they could never escape, picked through the mounds, looking for usable remnants that could be sold for survival. In these visits, I remember standing and watching, paralyzed by the reality that humans could permit other humans to live like this without a massive outcry. From society's point of view, there was really no difference between the garbage and the persons since all were worthless. But my most recent experience of this sense of horror was far closer to home—in Ossining, New York, just about forty minutes from where I grew up in New York City.

Our group wound through the dark, closed passages of Sing Sing Prison. Lines of men in jumpsuits, with a guard at each end, passed us. We were buzzed in through a greenish door, stepping suddenly into a huge open space, dimly lit. This was B Block, Building 5. As I struggled to get my bearings, I saw pallid green chain-link wire extending in front of me as far as I could see. The wire covered long, narrow walkways that surrounded the space, five stories up. As I looked into the wire at ground level, I could see a row of doors, each with a small barred window. Faces were pressed against some of them. Some uniformed men moved along the walkways, looking into windows and speaking loudly to whomever was behind the door. The noise was constant . . . multiple male voices, officers and inmates, always loud. As my ears adjusted, I could hear more intense conversation behind me, and I turned to watch the chaplain explaining our visit to the officers in what appeared to be a small guardroom. Some of the energy was familiar to me. I had been teaching weekly in a women's prison in Atlanta for many years and could navigate inmates and officers, always full of friendly greetings and firm speech tones. I was used to navigating the complex of low contemporary brick buildings at the edge of Atlanta, where I knew the suffering of the women inside and the injustices, both minor and major, they experienced in their lives.

B Block in Sing Sing was different. Partly it was the different intensity of men and the greater potential in the air for physical violence than I would ever experience in a women's prison. Partly it was the immense Victorian fortress of the prison itself, dark and decaying, and partly it was the sheer size of B Block, which ran the length and breadth of a football field, the height of one of the older New York City apartment buildings. It was laid out so that as guards walked down the center area, they could see every one of the several hundred inmates. Hundreds of men living on top of each other, yet each isolated in a tiny green cubicle, with a toilet and a cot. I felt the naked power of the place. No matter how humane any one person, officer or inmate, tried to be, Sing Sing simply blotted out humanity. Its purpose was to dehumanize.

Just like the garbage dump at Nanjido. The difference is that while Nanjido emerged without careful planning, as a by-product of rapid industrialization, economic growth, and inequality, Sing Sing is a planned structure, where the physical plant and the organization all emerged out of conscious decisions. When I say this, I do not mean that everything I saw is the result of a clear plan, since much of the institution has grown in response to the results of previous decisions and to changes in the surrounding social climate. But, nevertheless, these men have been placed purposely in this setting designed solely for their incarceration.

I make this distinction to begin my discussion about our Christian obligation to acknowledge and address the current U.S. prison situation, because the naming of specific obligations is at the heart of the heritage of progressive Christianity, whether embodied in the Social Gospel movement and its Social Creed of 1908 or in a speech of Martin Luther King Jr. Walter Rauschenbusch, a leader in the Social Gospel movement, wrote that "instead of a society resting on coercion, exploitation, and inequality, Jesus desired to found a society resting on love, service, and equality."[2] Jesus' call to realize this kingdom of God was, Rauschenbusch believed, the essence of Christianity and thus at the heart of all Christian discipleship. The call for justice present in this heritage assumes all persons are of value and thus gives rise to a corresponding obligation to address the situations where they are not valued. In the contemporary United States, prisons are one of the most challenging examples of how persons are not valued.

PRISONS IN THE UNITED STATES: AN ENDURING CRISIS

In previous centuries, those who committed crimes were given public physical punishment (such as whipping) and were rarely confined. In Puritan America these public punishments were understood as part of the theological order. Criminals were examples of inherently sinful humanity, whose public punishment would serve both as a means of reintegration and as a warning.[3] But treatment of criminals began to change with the Industrial Revolution, as the newly emerging cities brought large numbers of people into closer relationship, raising new fears and developing a new sense of criminals as a class. By the late eighteenth and early nineteenth centuries, prison buildings, usually resembling medieval fortresses, began to be built in the United States and Europe. Indeed, prison buildings were among the first capital projects of the new United States, with eleven states building prisons by 1800.[4] Punishing criminals was no longer a public event, where the criminal served as a warning example of a sinner. Instead, criminals were to be set apart, so they could not contaminate society. And instead of public physical punishment serving as a one-time means of absolution allowing reintegration into society, punishment was seen as a longer-term process that could reform or change a person.

As the vehicle for this kind of punishment, prisons were total institutions, designed to restructure a person's soul. The first prisons were designed for lives of complete silence and continuous hard labor. In Pennsylvania's Eastern State Penitentiary, which was considered the most ambitious and far-thinking experiment in punishment when it opened in 1829, prisoners lived in individual cells in total isolation. Cells had "feed doors" and private exercise areas to ensure that there would be no contact with other inmates and only limited contact with guards. If prisoners had to be moved, they wore dark hoods so they could neither see the faces of other prisoners or have their own face revealed. Living a combination of solitude and hard work, the prisoner was supposed to view this cell as "the beautiful gate of the Temple leading to a happy life and by a peaceful end, to Heaven."[5] By the end of the century, this religious framing of prison reform had shifted so that criminals were no longer sinners but sick individuals, yet the medical language was ambivalent. There could be an appeal to criminality as a disease that was able to be cured, or there could be an argument that a person's heredity made him or her simply unreformable.

In the one hundred years since the Social Creed, prisons have remained invisible from society, even from the view of society's reformers. In the period after World War I, crime in general (instead of the behavior of particular groups) began to emerge as a general issue.[6] In the postwar 1950s, a new cycle of fearful concern about crime started, which intensified in the 1960s and has continued steadily until today. A variety of social changes have maintained this fear, including (1) the impact of the Civil Rights Movement and the passage of the Civil Rights Act, which brought African Americans into new visibility through the guarantee of legal rights and provoked corresponding concerns among whites, often at an unconscious level; (2) increasingly unstable economic circumstances for working-class persons through loss of blue-collar industrial labor, an impact felt more heavily among white persons; (3) the creation of African American urban enclaves of poverty through shifts in employment, the suburban movements of both whites and upwardly mobile blacks, and urban redevelopment; and (4) the entrance into the United States of more powerful and addictive drugs, particularly cocaine.

These trends were channeled into prisons through the government's war on crime, particularly its war on drugs. Beginning as part of Lyndon Johnson's dream of the Great Society, this "war" has been carried out through the mechanisms of the criminal justice system. The old idea that imprisonment can potentially reform persons has virtually disappeared from public life. Instead, being "tough on crime" is a perennially popular position for politicians. Judicial discretion in sentencing has been severely limited through legislative actions enforcing sentencing frameworks such as "three strikes and you're out" or the "seven deadly sins," with particularly harsh sentences for drug convictions. These actions have been rooted in popular fears about crime strengthened by media images that have emphasized crimes committed by African Americans against Euro-Americans.

As a result, the number of incarcerated persons has steadily risen. By 1991 the United States had the highest incarceration rate of any nation in the world, a distinction it continues to hold.[7] In 1981, 1.8 million persons, out of 229.5 million persons in the United States, were under some form of correctional supervision, including probation, jail, prison, or parole. By 2005 this number is over 7 million, out of 281.4 million in the 2000 U.S. census.[8] Thus while the overall population grew by a little less than 25 percent, the number of persons incarcerated grew by almost 300 percent. Convictions for drug offenses grew by 37 percent between 1996 and 2002, contributing to the over 50 percent of the prison population convicted on a drug or violence charge. One-half of prison inmates were under the influence of drugs or alcohol when arrested (although this proportion represents a decrease since its high in 1996). These arrests and convictions have had the most impact on communities of color since approximately 64 percent of the prison population are ethnic minorities.[9] For African American men, the numbers are even more overwhelming; based on current rates of first incarceration, an estimated 32 percent of black males will enter state or federal prison during their lifetime, compared to 17 percent of Hispanic males and 5.9 percent of white males.[10]

While noting these changes, realize that many constants remain. One constant is that the majority of those classified as criminals are always from those classified as the poorest and most dislocated persons in society. Thus, at the end of the nineteenth century, prison reformer Zebulon Brockway wrote that the criminal population was "to a considerable extent the product of our civilization and also of emigration to our shore from the degenerated populations of crowded European marts."[11] The second constant is the disproportional presence of African Americans, despite the variable presence of other groups. Before the Civil War, few blacks were imprisoned because plantations administered their own punishments. This trend continued in the South where, immediately after the Civil War, convicted African Americans were not housed in prisons, but leased by states as farm labor, and later were the majority of prisoners in state-run chain gangs, abolished for their violent cruelty by the 1950s. The reality reflected by these constants includes both stigmatization (who is seen as inherently criminal) and lack of opportunity (who has access to resources of education, job opportunities, and housing that can guarantee stable livelihood), which have always affected one's chances of ending up a prisoner.

CHRISTIAN REFLECTION

Christian tradition, drawing upon its Jewish heritage, provides a basic warrant for obligation to those who are at the margins of the social order. Throughout the history of this Christian involvement, Matthew 25:31–46 has served as a source. The text even specifically mentions prisons: "I was sick and you took care of me, I was in prison and you visited me" (v. 36). However, the actual living out of this warrant has varied widely over the centuries. A constant moral question that has run through all of the differing forms of involvement has been how to draw boundaries around the marginalized. Tensions over this boundary can be seen most clearly in approaches to poverty as the Christian church struggled with the biblical notion of poverty as a virtue, a notion that was eclipsed with the rise of capitalism and the Protestant Reformation and modified into a boundary between deserving and undeserving poor. Christians have often felt obligations to help those seen as "deserving," that is, suffering through no fault of their own. This obligation weakens when dealing with those seen as "undeserving" or somehow responsible for their plight.

Prisoners have usually not been seen as part of the deserving poor, since they have broken the law. Before Christianity became the religion of the Roman Empire, divine justice could not be equivalent to human law, but once Christianity became the religion of the state, the two could be merged. If human law was analogous to the divine lawful order, breaking the law could be understood as committing sin. But even so, there was still the question of why punishment should be administered. Was it for the protection of the order of the state, or as a way of correcting a sinner? Augustine, one of the first to work on these issues theologically, distinguished between punishment as correction, done out of love, in imitation of divine punishment, and punishment as a human penalty required for civic order and the common good. Yet this distinction between human and divine has always been hard to make.

The Calvinist Puritan Christianity that shaped the founding of the United States was framed by the Augustinian heritage of sin and punishment. The social order was to be patterned as closely as possible on the divine order, with magistrates ruling in the name of God. While all were sinners, certain people who violated the divine order required punishment and "the more awesome the experience, the more valuable it could be as a means of humbling."[12] At different times and places, different strands of these moral theologies have been dominant. For example, puritanical notions of sin and the necessity of retribution have had a longer cultural history in the U.S. South than the North as they became entwined with concerns for racial and sexual purity in southern evangelical Protestantism.[13] Public discussion of punishment today continues to include a changing mix of vengeance and reform.

JUSTICE AND CHRISTIAN RESPONSIBILITY

Given this background and history, how might Christians think about their responsibility to incarcerate persons and act on that responsibility? The Social Creed for the Twenty-first Century promotes a social order built on the foundations of justice and peace. "Justice" and "peace" stand for our vision of the good society, an order where people can flourish as individuals and as a whole. It would be hard to argue that much peace or justice is found in our current prison system, so what can we do?

The first step is to consider the multiple aspects of justice. Justice can be seen as a question of *distribution* (on what basis are goods in society distributed?) or a question of *retribution* (where punishment must right or repay the disruption and damage that has been caused). An emphasis on distributive justice could lead to reflection on the unequal distribution of punishment in our society. Why have poor persons and persons of color consistently been overrepresented in the prison population and consistently received harsher and longer sentencing? A variety of studies show that minorities, particularly African American men, are more likely than European Americans to be arrested and, on conviction, given longer sentences or the death penalty.[14] Action to address these inequalities is likely to occur through advocacy in the public policy arena, and it can also lead to action engaging the broader social forces that shape the conditions of those who are poor and marginalized. What David Hilfiker calls the "extraordinary stresses" of communities of chronic poverty—the condition of living surrounded by broken-down facilities, inadequate education, and constant lack of jobs and economic resources—makes criminal behavior more likely and a more punitive reaction to that behavior equally likely.[15] Many if not most of those currently incarcerated have never had access to decent education, housing, or employment. If addicted to drugs or alcohol, they have had little possibility of access to rehabilitation programs. These inequalities are the conditions for the punitive cycles of unemployment and prison that afflict many Americans.

Justice as retribution requires some careful thinking. It is a form of justice found in every culture, embodied in the lines of Hebrew Scripture directing that there should be "eye for eye, tooth for tooth" (Exod 21:24) when adjudicating the results of violence. Its aim is to restore a previous balance that has been damaged by criminal action. When a violent crime is committed, we often hear that the perpetrators need to "get what they deserve." Certainly, it is not just to allow persons to suffer no consequences for acts that have caused harm to others. But we speak very little about what kinds of punishments really are deserved or do "fit the crime." Public conversation about the response to crime tends to fixate upon two alternatives—maximum punishment vs. no punishment—so that any reduction of the maximum penalty (such as the death penalty) is discussed as though the perpetrator has been released into freedom. Very little attention is paid to what might be the appropriate type and level of punishment, let alone what is our social responsibility to both offender and victim.

In the past few decades, more discussion of a third form of justice, restorative justice, has taken place as an alternative to the forms of retributive justice that currently shape our criminal justice system. While retributive justice looks back at the disrupted social order, restorative justice looks toward the future to consider the development of relationships that make possible a more peaceful community. While our current system focuses upon the state (which prosecutes crimes) and the offender (who is prosecuted), restorative justice focuses upon the restoration and healing of offender, victim, and community. Punishment does not focus on repayment by the offender, whether in terms of years in prison or payment of fines. While a restorative justice process could include these penalties, the focus is on repairing a broken relationship in ways that enable both victim and offender to be full participants and members of the community. Further, since the community has been violated, it is the community's obligation to engage in the work of restoration.

Processes of restorative justice can include victim support and advocacy, restitution, community service, victim impact panels, victim-offender mediation, circle sentencing, family group conferencing, community boards that meet with offenders to determine appropriate sanctions, victim empathy classes for offenders, and community policing. These practices contrast with the customary working of the criminal justice system where the focus is on the offender, the victim is invisible, and the community is represented by law. A variety of community-based programs around the country are working to incorporate practices of restorative justice in schools and communities, and in the criminal justice system.

For example, some counties in Minnesota have developed processes of alternative sentencing that enabled a woman convicted of embezzlement due to a gambling addiction to receive psychiatric help, enter a mediation process with those victimized, and work out a repayment plan.[16] In Canada, restorative justice circles may be used with young offenders who encounter a mediated group meeting where the youth recount what happened and then hear those affected talk about the impact of the crime. An observer of one such circle described how one boy "between sobs, spoke of how he felt, that it was intended as a prank, a joke but that it was not a joke." He then had to hear the girl who had been dragged by a car down the street in the "prank" speak of her ongoing fear of walking at night. A punishment was negotiated that included participation in a traveling high school production teaching students to consider risks involved in decisions.[17]

New ways of thinking about justice offer a vision of possible alternatives, enabling us to imagine something else instead of—or, at least, in addition to—our current harsh legal system. Restorative justice is particularly valuable for working with young offenders, such as the young men in the example above, because it encourages accountability, offers supervision, and avoids the segregation of a juvenile justice facility, where criminal behavior may be fostered rather than prevented.

WHAT NOW?

There are multiple ways for U.S. Christians to engage the prison system at all its phases and levels. There can be a focus on preventive measures, such as sponsorship of a program offering mentoring and support for poor youth or lobbying for better public educational provisions. There can be political engagement around current practices of arrests and sentencing procedures. Or there can be work with or on behalf of those currently incarcerated, such as lobbying for support for educational programs in prisons or volunteering to teach or counsel inmates. One direction that is emerging as an important area in prison-related work is support for reentry programs. Higher incarceration rates over the past decades are leading to higher reentry numbers. Prisoners often are released with no more resources in funding and skills than they had when they entered—and, if they were incarcerated for reasons related to addiction, little access to services that can support continued sobriety. Political work must be done to support legislation that provides greater resources for reentry services, and on-the-ground work is required to support the few existing programs through the kinds of support networks that congregations are particularly able to provide.

A recent article on U.S. prisons by the U.S. program director for Human Rights Watch was titled "U.S. Addiction to Incarceration Puts 2.3 Million in Prison."[18] To call actions "addictions" is to say that the behavior is irrational, harmful to the self and others, and yet driven by what seems to be an inescapable desire. Christians need not—indeed should not—be these kinds of persons. We have much work to do.

QUESTIONS FOR DISCUSSION

1. What are the lenses of justice you believe should be brought to prison issues? How would you balance concern for retributive, distributive, and restorative justice? What are other values Christians should use when reflecting on prisons? Equality? Compassion?
2. What do you think should be the task of prison: To control crime? To punish criminals? To offer rehabilitation? If rehabilitation is one of the functions of prison, what kinds of programs do you think would be important?
3. Do you believe imprisonment is just? Are there other ways of justly dealing with those who have broken the law, particularly those who have caused harm to others? If punishment is in itself just, how might persons be justly sentenced? What might a just prison look like?
4. What kinds of involvement do you think Christians are obliged to have in relation to prisons? What might you plan for yourself and/or your congregation?

RESOURCES

Books

Elsner, Alan. *Gates of Injustice: The Crisis in America's Prisons*. Upper Saddle River, NJ: Prentice-Hall, 2006.

Magnani, Laura, and Harmon L. Wray. *Beyond Prisons: A New Interfaith Paradigm for Our Failed Prison System*. Minneapolis: Fortress, 2006.

Pierce, Dennis. *Prison Ministry: Hope behind the Wall*. New York: Haworth Pastoral Press, 2006.

Prejean, Helen. *Dead Man Walking*. New York: Vintage, 1994.

Zehr, Howard. *The Little Book of Restorative Justice*. Intercourse, PA: Good Books, 2002.

Web Sites

Restorative Justice Consortium, http://www.restorativejustice.org.uk.

The Roundtable on Religion and Social Welfare Policy, http://www.religionandsocialpolicy.org/resources/fbprison_programs.cfm.

The Sentencing Project, http://www.sentencingproject.org.
Urban Institute, http://www.urban.org/justice/index.cfm.

NOTES

1. Note that Nanjido closed down in 1993 and has been shaped into five theme parks (http://english.seoul.go.kr/today/about/about_02top_5501.htm).
2. Walter Rauschenbusch, *Christianity and the Social Crisis* (1907; Louisville, KY: Westminster/John Knox Press, 1991), 70.
3. Lawrence Friedman, *Crime and Punishment in American History* (New York: Basic Books, 1994), 25–33.
4. Scott Christianson, *With Liberty for Some: 500 Years of Imprisonment in America* (Boston: Northeastern University Press, 2000), 101.
5. Quotation from Charles Dickens's tour of Eastern State in *American Notes for General Circulation*, cited in Christianson, *With Liberty for Some*, 134.
6. Friedman, *Crime and Punishment in American History*, 273.
7. Christianson, *With Liberty for Some*, 285.
8. http://www.npg.org/facts/us_historical_pops.htm, BJS; http://www.ojp.usdoj.gov/bjs/glance/corr2.htm.
9. http://www.ojp.usdoj.gov/bjs/crimoff.htm#inmates.
10. Ibid.
11. Zebulon Brockway, "The Incorrigible Criminal: What Is He and How Should He Be Treated?" *Proceedings of the National Prison Association* (1884): 105–12; cited in Christianson, *With Liberty for Some*, 180.
12. Cited in Gail Sussman Marcus, "'Due Execution of the General Rules of Righteousness': Criminal Procedure in New Haven Town and Colony, 1638–1658," in David D. Hall et al., eds., *Saints and Revolutionaries: Essays in Early American History* (New York: Norton, 1984), 129–30.
13. See Donald G. Mathews, "The Southern Rite of Human Sacrifice," *Journal of Southern Religion*, August 22, 2000, http://jsr.fsu.edu/mathews.htm.
14. For excellent information on these disparities, see the work of the Sentencing Project, http://www.sentencingproject.org.
15. David Hilfiker, *Urban Injustice: How Ghettoes Happen* (New York: Seven Stories Press, 2003), 4.
16. Robert Franklin, "City Uses 'Restorative Justice' with Woman Who Stole to Gamble," *Star Tribune*, July 26, 1995, http://www.doc.state.mn.us/rj/documents/CityusesRJwithwomanwhostoletogamble_000.pdf.
17. See http://www.crcna.org/pages/oct2002_vanderberg.cfm.
18. Jamie Fellner, "U.S. Addiction to Incarceration Puts 2.3 Million in Prison," Dec. 1, 2006, http://hrw.org/english/docs/2006/12/01/usdom14728.htm.

Chapter 5

For Public Education That Practices and Promotes Peace

MARCIA Y. RIGGS

I was born in the late 1950s to college-educated parents who taught in the public schools and were lay leaders in our local church. In my black middle-class family comprising two parents and five children, we were taught to be God-fearing, and the values of honesty, diligence, commitment, integrity, hard work, and perseverance in the midst of adversity were to be expressions of love for God, self, and others. I was born into racially segregated circumstances and nurtured during my formative years by a suburban black community in Salisbury, Maryland, that included black teachers (public and Sunday school), black doctors, black preachers, and black neighborhood storekeepers. In those circumstances, it felt like everyone with whom I was in contact was on my side—even when they disciplined me. My parents, the church, and the public school teachers all cared about me and had educational aspirations for me as well as a commitment to my becoming a good human being. They had a stake in my knowing right from wrong, in my understanding that actions had consequences, and in my caring about the feelings as well as the needs of others.

After moving to rural North Carolina in 1968, I walked into an integrated classroom taught by a white female teacher. For the first time, I felt vulnerable in a context where I previously had felt affirmed and cared for by adults. In this new, integrated circumstance, the synergy between my family, my church, and the public schools began to break down. There was a feeling that relationships between some very important people in my life had been disrupted. I could no longer expect to have many of the same people interacting in the different contexts of my life. The public educational context became a place where I went to get "book learning" rather than another space where care for my whole self (mind, body, and spirit) happened.

In 2005, my ten-year-old godson and his grandmother came to live with me in Georgia. Of course, one of the first matters was to register him in the elementary school. When I bought my home, I went looking for a good neighborhood, which for me looked much like the ones in which I grew up (except that there was to be racial-ethnic diversity among the neighbors): hard-working, middle-class folks seeking home ownership and to create a safe community in which to raise families and retire. I assumed that because the neighborhood met these broad criteria the neighborhood public school would be fine.

I was wrong. The school is overcrowded and underfunded; my godson's classroom was a trailer (without a bathroom) on the back lot. His teacher seemed to be nice and qualified, but she did not have any patience, particular skills, or training to teach this child with learning disabilities. After several attempts to communicate with her and several demeaning notes to my godson about his inability to do what was asked of him in class, his grandmother withdrew him from the school and decided to homeschool him. This step was a rude awakening for his grandmother and me, who were graduates of the public school system all those years ago. My godson is fortunate because his grandmother and I have college and postgraduate degrees; he can receive a quality education at home. But this is not how it should be—should it?

These stories serve as a lens for the discussion of the interaction of race, gender, and economic class as social processes that impact and inform public policy on public education. Although these anecdotes reflect the policy concerns of two different eras, with my story demonstrating the effects of the *Brown v. Board of Education* decision's concern that integration be implemented "with all deliberate speed" and my godson's story pointing us toward contemporary policy concerns of "no child left behind," both stories are representative of the failures of and hopes for public education in this country. Living in this country, having the freedom to make educational choices based on philosophical or religious grounds is part of how we understand our democratic society. However, a forced choice to homeschool a child because the public education system is inadequate is also a corruption of that same democratic society. Our stories press the following questions:

- Is not an earmark of a democratic society its ability to educate all of its children?

- Shouldn't public education for all children be an outward sign of how well U.S. society is providing a context for life, liberty, and the pursuit of happiness for all of its citizens?
- How have the failures of public education become an outward sign of the moral corruption of our democratic ethos?

FROM "WITH ALL DELIBERATE SPEED" TO "NO CHILD LEFT BEHIND"

In this section, I draw descriptive connections between my story and my godson's story by highlighting some interconnecting public education policy decisions from 1954 through 2002. The policies that I highlight are critical markers as to how we have sought to allay the moral corruption of our democratic ethos with legislation that addresses some of the most contentious features and fears of our life together in the United States: racial discrimination, sexual discrimination, economic inequalities, discrimination based on physical and mental disabilities, and xenophobia. The policy decisions that I have chosen to stress point to what I ultimately describe as fissures and a fault in public education policy.

Let's begin with the *Brown* decision. There are actually two decisions in the landmark Supreme Court ruling in *Brown v. Board of Education* (1954–1955). The first decision, on May 17, 1954, declared that state-sanctioned segregation of public schools is a violation of the Fourteenth Amendment. The second decision, on May 31, 1955, is the one best remembered because of its wording; this final decision regarding timing and implementation ordered desegregation with "all deliberate speed."[1] Although race is at the heart of *Brown,* the decisions in *Brown* establish two important features upon which subsequent public policy regarding education is grounded. First, public education policy is corrective; education is an institution of the society that socializes children to become citizens. If public education legislation does not seek to secure everyone's equal right to education by correcting for past and present unjust educational practices, then the democratic ideal of equality would become so diminished that we could not expect any loyalty from our citizens or make honest claims about being a democracy. Second, public education policy is (re)distributive; education is an institution of the society that prepares the country's labor force and thus is a means by which human and economic resources are (re)distributed in society. Without the *Brown* decisions establishing such corrective and (re)distributive parameters, public education policy may not have gone in the directions that I describe below.

On April 9, 1965, President Lyndon Johnson signed the Elementary and Secondary Education Act (ESEA) into law. ESEA was part of President Johnson's "War on Poverty" and was to provide substantial monetary funds for K–12 education to schools serving children from low-income families. The funds were to provide for professional development of teachers, instructional materials, resources to support educational programs, and parental involvement. This law was originally authorized through 1970, and it has been reauthorized every five years since with the basic goal that targeted government resources help to provide disadvantaged students with access to a quality public education.[2] The current reauthorization of this act is the No Child Left Behind Act of 2001 (NCLB) signed into law by President George W. Bush in 2002.

The overall intent of the NCLB is "for all students—regardless of economic status, race, ethnicity, language spoken at home, or disability—to attain proficiency in reading, math, and science by 2014."[3] This legislation emphasizes standards, testing, accountability measures, and teacher quality. When I think about No Child Left Behind as the continuation of ESEA and its grounding premises as those of the nation's "War on Poverty," I am immediately struck by the way that my educational experience in rural North Carolina was enhanced because the earlier policies were informed by a larger social agenda that had to do with quality-of-life issues. I am not sure what the larger social agenda of NCLB is in terms of how money is actually being spent to enrich the educational experience of my godson's peers. Is the larger social agenda of NCLB driven by an economics of profit rather than an economics of justice and care? An emphasis on raising test scores in science and math seems to suggest a concern with gaining a competitive edge in the global marketplace. I certainly understand the need for a citizenry that has technological acumen, but what is the larger socio-moral vision guiding the education of our children so that they are responsible creators and consumers of technological advances that are the earmark of twenty-first-century life? What kind of persons are we educating our children to be, not simply what are our children being educated to do?

Likewise, because disadvantage in public education has not been and is not solely a function of economic discrimination, a few other important education policies must be noted as critical keys for unlocking the fissures and fault in education policy on the way to fulfilling *Brown* and living into NCLB. Of particular interest are several policies that point to an expanding concept of discrimination that has been a part of the evolution of education policy.

Title IX of the Education Amendments of 1972 and Section 504 and Title II of the Americans with Disabilities Act target sex discrimination and discrimination against disabled students. The Office of Civil Rights (OCR) enforces these laws by investigating and resolving complaints that are filed and by initiating reviews of recipients of federal funding for the purpose of ensuring compliance.[4] In 2000, the OCR enforcement of Section 504 was extended to focus on providing educational services to students with Acquired Immune Deficiency Syndrome (AIDS). This enforcement of Section 504 specifies that children with AIDS are handicapped persons (1) who are entitled to attend school in the regular classroom, (2) whose evaluation and placement must have procedural safeguards, and (3) who have right to confidentiality.[5] Finally, Title VI of the Civil

Rights Acts of 1964 is concerned overall with prohibiting discrimination on the basis of race, color, or national origin in the operation of any federally assisted programs. In the 1970s, compliance reviews were conducted in school districts with large Spanish-surnamed student populations, and a number of common practices that have a discriminatory effect on educational opportunity for Spanish-surnamed students were found. Such discrimination was also found with regard to other national-origin minority groups such as Chinese and Portuguese students. Common practices underlying the discrimination are failure to provide English language instruction, assignment to classes for the mentally retarded and denial to college preparatory classes, ability or group tracking for purposes other than increasing English language proficiency, and failure to provide notices to parents in a language other than English.[6]

What these laws represent is an evolution of education policy that embraces an expanding concept of discrimination that is important to a discussion of public education policy and the moral corruption of our democratic ethos. These laws point to the idea that the way we embody our democracy—physically, mentally, linguistically—is critical. I cannot overlook the connection between embodiment and the practices of a democracy as just or unjust when I think about my story and my godson's story. We embody race, gender, and mental disabilities that could render us outside of the moral community, and thus expendable, except for such legislation. So, with the conviction that legislation is sometimes the only means to secure the viability of our democratic ethos, I turn to a discussion of the fissures and fault in current public education policy.

FISSURES AND A FAULT IN CURRENT PUBLIC EDUCATION POLICY

Public response to No Child Left Behind has included the following criticisms: (a) the accountability imperative of NCLB is important but too narrow in that a single test is used to determine school performance; (b) where there is broader community support there is shared responsibility for schools, and NCLB has no specific means for attaining such; (c) when schools are labeled "in need of improvement," those schools are abandoned by some higher-performing students, teachers, and the communities; and (d) strong focus on a single high-stakes test is creating deep anxiety for students or even causing some students to drop out of school. Public recommendations to improve NCLB include:

- Low-performing schools should have resources directed to them along with a mandated set of strategies and interventions for improvement, and not just punitive sanctions.
- The accountability gap might be addressed by including a value-added assessment system along with single-test criterion.

- Supplemental educational services might prevent students transferring and target student outcomes.
- Improved academic supports should be made available to students, including health and mental health services, social services, mentoring, a safe environment for tutoring, and after-school enrichment opportunities.[7]

Most important, the public knows that we (students, parents, and community members) have a critical role to play in the reauthorization process and implementation of NCLB. Based upon these criticisms and recommendations, the fissures in public education policy signal the places where we may be able to reverse the moral corruption of our democratic ethos before our efforts have the effect of evermore diminishing returns.

Whereas the public's criticism of NCLB points to fissures in current public education policy, the Supreme Court's recent decision in *Parents Involved in Community Schools v. Seattle School District No. 1 et al.* earmarks a fault. On June 28, 2007, in a 5–4 decision the Supreme Court ruled against racial balancing plans for public schools. The decision struck down plans in Seattle, Washington, and Louisville, Kentucky. Chief Justice Roberts maintained that the historical precedent of *Brown* necessitated that race not be used to assign children to schools even for the very different reasons offered by the schools for such plans today. Justice Kennedy was the swing vote of the majority opinion; he spoke against the categorical opposition to such plans voiced by Chief Justice Roberts. Kennedy asserted that plans should seek to ensure diversity with regard to a school's racial makeup within a district rather than with regard to the placement of individual students; for example, school officials might make strategic decisions about where to build a school to affect diversity.[8]

The fissures of NCLB education policy indicate the ways in which our national ideals about equality continue to disturb our national consciousness so that we are compelled to put in place policy that has admirable, even democratizing goals. The fault exposed by the recent Supreme Court decision is that although we now seem willing to concede that race matters, we are still on a quest for race-neutral (at best) and colorblind (at worst) policy that will nurture authentic diversity in U.S. society. We seem unable to develop a national conscience (in the matured persistent moral sense) that prods us into making consistent hard ethical choices that ensure the viability of the policy's democratizing goals and a larger moral vision of diversity.

In order to position ourselves as a society to determine and make hard ethical choices about public education policy, we need to question our economic priorities as military spending escalates to support war efforts while funds for life-support services are being cut off or dwindling rapidly. As many other chapters in this book demonstrate, in addition to a seriously underfunded public education system, we also face unconscionable problems regarding health insurance for children, assistance for survivors of Hurricane Katrina, minimum wage, and social security. If we as a nation are willing to ask and seek answers to difficult questions about our priorities, we might begin to develop a national conscience (in the matured persistent moral sense of the word) that will helpfully inform public education policy.

VIOLENCE AND JUST PEACE AS TERMS OF THE DEBATE

From a faith-based perspective that reflects a communal interest in the well-being of our nation's children, it is time to rethink a progressive Christian approach to public policy. From this perspective, the terms of public policy need to be reframed. The terms derive for me from the Christian social gospel, black religious radicalism, and liberation roots that inform my understanding of faith. However, these terms also represent a needful posture of healthy twenty-first-century Christians—that is, Christian faith seeking to speak to other religious faiths in the context of U.S. democratic pluralism, thus faith-based. The two terms that drive this reframing of the goals of public education policy are violence and just peace.

In the classic text *Religion and Violence*, Robert McAfee Brown pushes us to move beyond the conventional definition of violence as an overt physical act of destruction to whatever violates the other person or persons in the sense of infringing upon or disregarding or abusing or denying the "Other," whether physical harm is involved or not. Succinctly, violence may be defined as the violation of personhood, an act that transforms persons into things.[9] Within this understanding, social injustice is an act of violence because it occurs when institutional structures of a society operate in ways that destroy human hope and possibilities and objectify people seeking to live within those structures. When public education policy actually produces such debilitating anxiety in students because they are only being taught to pass a test that they choose to drop out, then that policy perpetuates education as violence. There is mostly a covert rather than an overt quality to the social injustice in education as just described, but there may also be an overt physical component whenever inadequate physical facilities are a result of the failure to fund schools properly or to provide safe environments for learning.

McAfee Brown also noted that "disinformation" is a key feature of the U.S. context; disinformation has to do with a willingness on the part of public officials to tell lies that manipulate facts and us.[10] As the public's response to NCLB points to an accountability gap and procedures that misinform parents about services available to their children, disinformation is another way that current public education policy promotes violence. For example, in the state of Georgia, legislation has been passed that will allow students to attend public schools online. My godson's grandmother stumbled upon this recent decision as she was constructing his homeschool curriculum for this year. His grandmother prides herself on staying abreast of educational legislation and services, so she was shocked to have missed this. Two things come to mind with reference to the violence of disinformation.[11] First, the grandmother has had ongoing contact with the Board of Education's division that oversees homeschooling, and no one ever mentioned this recent option. Second, although this is supposed to be public education online, there does not seem to be free full access for any child. In other words, you cannot simply enroll in online public education in a manner similar to registering your child in the neighborhood public school. The potential for online public education to serve the democratizing goals of current policy is being subverted, and violence becomes embedded in the policy.

If inquiry into the violence of public education policy itself becomes the subject of political discourse and policy making, might we begin to find more authentic ways to narrow the educational gap between privileged and disadvantaged students as well as open a window onto why violence in the schools exists? In other words, a public education policy that perpetrates covert and overt violence provides the ground for violence within the context of the schools themselves. We cannot foster educational contexts that are nonviolent (do not objectify our children and assault their personhood) while simultaneously enacting education policies that perpetrate violence against our children. If education in U.S. society is supposed to be one way to offer equal opportunity to our citizens, how do we diminish the social injustice of current public education policy that corrupts this value? Thus, two final questions for this discussion: How do we describe and enact a democratic U.S. society that will educate well all of its children and truly be a context for life, liberty, and pursuit of happiness for all its citizens? What can we in the churches do?

In 1999, the World Council of Churches (WCC) adopted the "Decade to Overcome Violence." The Decade runs 2001 through 2010; the focus is structural or systemic violence in political, economic, racial, and gender relationships. The core assumption of the WCC's mandate is that peacemaking must be at the core of the life and witness of the churches.[12] Peace is understood here not via the negative as the absence of conflict and violence but in the affirmative as the presence of just social relations. Biblically, such a vision of just peace is expressed by the Hebrew word *shalom*, interpreted as "communal well-being in which God's creation is justly ordered" as well as those things to which Jesus alludes when he looks at the corruption, abuse of power, and violence in Jerusalem and says, "If only you knew today the things that make for peace."[13]

We in the churches must live into the vision of the WCC's Decade to Overcome Violence with respect to public education. Our faith-based advocacy for public education must not begin and end with after-school programs or with the promotion of Christian values through the teaching of Bible in the schools or with withdrawal into independent Christian schools. Faith-based advocacy for public education in the twenty-first century must surely have a twofold purpose. The first purpose is to become a place where the community can gather to discuss what is going on in the local schools in light of the diversity of faith confessions represented in the community. The churches must be places where congregants are nurtured to become partners in "ecumenical political dialogue."[14] Congregants involved in education—teachers, students, parents, Board of Education members, school counselors, and so forth—must be encouraged through Bible study as well as the worship life of the church to act as citizens motivated by the ethical and social implications of their religious beliefs. The second purpose is to witness for nonviolence. Perhaps it is time to enact strategies of nonviolent resistance to get the attention of policymakers and to reawaken all of us as to the failures of public education as acts of violence. Instead of reacting to the violence of a Columbine after the fact, it is time for people of faith to be proactive catalysts for a social climate of nonviolence. How about organizing as a regularly planned event on the church's monthly calendar a march, rally, or fair for just peace? How about some ecumenical and interfaith events sharing the wisdom of our traditions on just peace?

We in the churches must enter public debate about public education policy sharing biblical narratives and images of *shalom* as the means for offering a critique of the practices and a vision for the goals underlying such policy. Biblical narratives and images of *shalom* include turning swords into plowshares, lions dwelling with lambs, nations not studying war, fulfillment of the Year of Jubilee with Christ, and Christ as our *shalom* breaking down all dividing walls of hostility. From the perspective of biblical *shalom*, the practices of public education policy should not render schools within districts or all schools within the nation competitors for inadequate federal funding on the basis of test scores. Likewise, *shalom* accountability requires partnership at the federal and local levels because we acknowledge that we all benefit when our nation's children are educated well. Using biblical *shalom* to think about the moral vision needed to sustain the goals of public education policy means seeking to determine interrelated goals that create an educated citizenry who act on behalf of the sustainability of the earth; have technological wisdom and not just technical skills; practice transformative conflict as a way of living in a multicultural society and world; and speak truth to economic, political, social, racial, and gender injustices wherever they are found.

QUESTIONS FOR DISCUSSION

1. What do our national spending habits tell us about the state of the character (social values) of our democratic society?
2. How has equality become a commodity that we think we can manufacture—for example, through the testing strategies of education policy such as NCLB? Or, when will we develop an expanded sense

of equality that can accommodate multicultural conditions (pluralities of peoples, religions, etc.) of the society that we are, rather than some mythic ideal of an American society?

3. How are the ways in which we live together through public policy decisions often ways of perpetrating acts of violence?
4. Can we be a society that practices just peace?

RESOURCES

Books

Kozol, Jonathan. *The Shame of the Nation: The Restoration of Apartheid Schooling in America*. New York: Crown, 2005.

Meier, Deborah, and George Wood, eds. *Many Children Left Behind: How the No Child Left Behind Act Is Damaging Our Children and Our Schools.* Boston: Beacon Press, 2004.

Sunderman, Gail L., James S. Kim, and Gary Orfield. *NCLB Meets School Realities: Lessons from the Field.* Thousand Oaks, CA: Corwin Press, 2005.

Web Sites

The Center for Public Education, http://www.centerforpubliceducation.org.
National Priorities Project, http://www.nationalpriorities.org.
U.S. Department of Education, http://www.ed.gov.

NOTES

1. This discussion of *Brown v. Board of Education* is informed by a paper presented by Barbara A. Holmes, J.D., Ph.D., and Hon. Susan R. Holmes Winfield, associate judge, Superior Court of the District of Columbia, entitled "*Brown v. Board of Education*: A Retrospective" at the American Academy of Religion Conference in November 2004.
2. Pamela Karwasinski and Katharine Shek, "A Guide to the No Child Left Behind Act," http://www.centerforpubliceducation.org.
3. Ibid.
4. See http://www.ed.gov/print/about/offices/list/ocr/docs/tix_dis.html (accessed on August 13, 2007).
5. See http://www.ed.gov/print/about/offices/list/ocr/docs/hq53e9.html (accessed on August 13, 2007).
6. See http://www.ed.gov/print/about/offices/list/ocr/docs/nationaloriginmemo .html (accessed on August 13, 2007).
7. See http://www.publiceducation.org/2006_NCLB_National_Report.pdf (accessed on July 3, 2007).
8. See http://www.supremecourtus.gov/supremecourtopinions/06slipopinion.html/ (accessed on July 12, 2007); http://www.cnn.com/LAW/ (accessed on July 12, 2007); http://usatoday.com (accessed on July 12, 2007).

9. Robert McAfee Brown, *Religion and Violence*, 2nd ed. (Philadelphia: Westminster Press, 1987), 7.
10. Ibid., xvii–xix.
11. I am extending McAfee Brown's concept of disinformation to include actions by public officials and through public policy that are acts of deception, both intentionally and unintentionally. Acts of deception conceal from and/or present something as one thing while it actually functions another way to the public. In the example that follows, I think the failure of public officials to use all available means (such as public service ads) to inform the public of the new legislation and the use of a tedious entrance exam to enroll in the online public education are acts of deception that embody the violence of disinformation.
12. For specifics, see Richard D. N. Dickinson, "Overcoming Violence: A Historical Reflection on the Decade to Overcome Violence," *Ecumenical Review* 55, no. 3 (July 2003): 192–225.
13. Susan Thistlethwaite, ed., *A Just Peace Church* (Cleveland: United Church Press, 1986), 9.
14. Michael J. Perry, *Love and Power: The Role of Religion and Morality in American Politics* (New York: Oxford University Press, 1991), chap. 6.

Chapter 6

For Healing and Wholeness

AANA MARIE VIGEN

Meet Linda Miller, a Chicagoan who had health insurance until 2000 when Ameritech laid off its employees.[1] For as long as she could, Linda continued Ameritech's health coverage using COBRA, a federal law that enables former employees to retain their employment-based health policies for eighteen to thirty-six months—as long as they are able to pay the premium themselves. Unfortunately, Linda then discovered she had breast cancer. She was working, but uninsured and now carried the label "pre-existing condition." When she found permanent employment, the company's insurance plan refused to cover her cancer care. Linda describes her predicament:

> I couldn't get public assistance because you have to have a serious illness *and* be unemployed. I'd had temp jobs, and the fact that I worked was held against me. But if I don't work, how do I take care of myself? . . . I have a new job, but its insurance won't cover my cancer. Bill collectors call. I have no idea how I can pay them. I think of those years when I was healthy and paid for insurance and didn't even go to the doctor. Now that I need some help, I can't get it.

It doesn't seem fair, does it? Linda paid deductibles and co-payments for years, but was left without coverage when she most needed it. Linda's story is not unique. Forty-seven million Americans are without health insurance. This basic fact—a lack of affordable, high-quality care for all—presents people of faith with a pressing moral dilemma. What does it mean to love our sick or uninsured neighbor as ourselves? In this chapter, I invite you to wrestle with some ugly facts about U.S. healthcare that force us to rethink what we mean by valuing human life and dignity.

THE DISCONCERTING FACE OF U.S. HEALTHCARE

Uninsured, Underinsured, and Impoverished

Per 2006 U.S. Census data, 15.8 percent of legal U.S. inhabitants have no health insurance. More children (8.7 million total) are uninsured than there were in 2005. Minnesota has the lowest uninsured rate of any state (8.5 percent) while Texas has the highest (24.1 percent); thus, nearly one in four Texans has no insurance. Forty-seven million uninsured equals the cumulative population of twenty-four states plus the District of Columbia.[2] The United States is the only industrialized nation not to offer comprehensive health coverage to all of its citizens, and we are by far the richest nation in the world—the sole superpower.

Many pernicious myths persist about the uninsured: They don't work and are destitute, or conversely they are wealthy and can afford to pay privately for their care; they can get care when they really need it and at no cost to them; they are mostly illegal immigrants. In truth, eight out of ten uninsured Americans come from a working family, and two-thirds of the uninsured are from low-income (but not necessarily "officially poor") families; 79 percent are American citizens. Over a third of the uninsured postpone or neglect medical care needs, and when they do go for care, they are billed and pay out of pocket.[3] Most of the uninsured, along with a significant number who are insured, cannot afford the high costs, and many—uninsured *and* insured—file for personal bankruptcy as a result.

There is more to the uninsured story: the Census Bureau does not count the millions who are underinsured. If you are insured sporadically in a given year, you count as insured. To be "underinsured" means that you are insured only part of a year, or that you have some insurance but it does not adequately meet your health needs (the coverage is too limited or too expensive, the deductibles are too high, or all of the above). A June 2005 Commonwealth Fund study estimates that 16 million U.S. adults are underinsured and go without needed medical care, including important tests, drugs, treatments, and follow-up care.[4] The underinsured often make too much money to qualify for government assistance or insurance programs. Thus, when they get sick and seek care, they are at great financial risk—left with massive medical bills and a lot of stress not only about their health, but about how they will pay what they owe.

While being under- or uninsured in the United States afflicts the middle classes as well, a strong correlation exists between poverty and a lack of health coverage. According to 2006 Census data, 24.9 percent of households with an annual income of $25,000 or less had no health insurance. To be counted as "officially poor," you have to meet financial limits determined by the federal or state governments. In 2006, a family with two adults and two children under eighteen years of age could earn no more than $20,444 (a single adult could earn no more than $10,488) to be counted by the federal government as poor. Being counted is the key to Medicaid eligibility. Currently, 12.3 percent of the U.S. population (36.5 million people) are officially poor. Millions more subsist near this threshold in unofficial poverty and receive little or no government assistance.

Racial-Ethnic Inequalities in Health and Healthcare

While people of every race and ethnicity suffer from poverty and a lack of health insurance, a disproportionate number of Latino and black Americans, relative to their overall population, confront these twin hardships. Per 2006 Census data, Latino Americans make up 14.5 percent of the general population, and 34 percent of Latinos are uninsured. (The U.S. Census only counts legal inhabitants.) Black Americans represent 12 percent of the U.S. population, and 24 percent of blacks are poor. In contrast, 10.8 percent of non-Hispanic whites are uninsured and 8.2 percent are impoverished, while they compose 67 percent of the overall population. The burden of being uninsured or living in poverty is not distributed proportionately or fairly across racial-ethnic groups.

Moreover, Americans are not all equally healthy. Black Americans on average live fewer years than white Americans and have higher infant mortality rates. Black women are the least likely to get breast cancer of any racial-ethnic group, but if they do, they are the most likely to die from it. Alarmingly in Chicago, black women are 73 percent more likely to die of breast cancer than white women.[5] Linda Miller, the woman whose story began this chapter, is African American.

Furthermore, people of color often receive no or late treatment/screenings for health problems and less follow-up care than whites. They are also more likely than whites to live in heavily polluted areas and to have less access to affordable, healthy food. Transportation to medical care and language barriers are also serious problems. Sometimes patients of color are stereotyped and suffer because of assumptions that care providers unwittingly make about them.

Some argue that racial-ethnic inequalities are sporadic and uncommon. The U.S. Congress commissioned the prestigious Institute of Medicine (IOM) to explore this issue. The IOM concluded that there is a systemic problem and that communities of color "tend to receive a lower quality of healthcare than non-minorities, even when *access-related factors, such as patients' insurance status and income, are controlled*" (emphasis added). The IOM also found that communities of color experience "stereotyping, bias, and uncertainty on the part of healthcare providers" which "can all contribute to unequal treatment."[6] Indeed, the roots of racial-ethnic health and healthcare inequities are complex and multilayered, yet too many Americans of relative racial or socioeconomic privilege are unaware of the harsh realities that people of color confront routinely. That needs to change if we are sincere in our calling as Christians to protect life and to love our neighbors as ourselves.

Medical Research and Racial-Ethnic Inequalities

The roots of contemporary racial-ethnic inequalities in U.S. medical care run long and deep. One reason that we as a society do not always see them now is because we have repeatedly missed them in earlier historical moments. The notorious Tuskegee Syphilis Study (1932–1972) was neither the beginning nor the end of unethical medical and research practices. Colonial slaves were experimented upon without their consent and their cadavers stolen for study. Over time and through avoidance, denial, and a simple lack of awareness, our collective ethical vision has become (mis)shaped by a kind of moral astigmatism. By learning this history and asking critical and self-reflective questions about the present, we can correct our flawed vision, make amends to those harmed, and seek more just practices, laws, and structures.

The pertinent question is whether such unethical research practices could still take place today. Unfortunately, there are reasons for concern. For example, from 1988 to 2002, hundreds of HIV-positive foster children across the nation, approximately 465 living in New York City alone, participated in clinical drug trials. They did so without having independent advocates.[7] Some children experienced severe side effects from the drugs, more so than from the standard treatment that they received prior to the study—nausea and vomiting, weight loss, lack of energy, strength, and so on. In two cases in New York, foster parents stopped giving the drug to the children for fear it was harming them. In these cases, the children were removed from the foster homes and placed in group-home settings where the drug trial continued.[8]

Undeniably, discovering new and better drugs to treat awful diseases is vital. However, it is also significant that 99 percent of these foster children in New York City were Latino or African American and that they had no independent advocate who could remove them from the study. The city agency that made the deal to conduct this research was also their legal guardian.

Overall, we in the United States (and internationally) don't have a great track record of socioeconomic or racial-ethnic equality in medical research arenas. Artificial reproductive technologies such as in vitro fertilization, egg donation, and surrogacy are not covered by Medicaid or even by many private insurance plans. To a large degree, only the affluent can afford them. In contrast, impoverished women of color are often the ones who agree to be surrogates while young women struggling to pay for college are recruited to be egg donors. The first AIDS drugs were tested on Africans who were later denied access to the approved drug therapies with the argument that it would not be cost effective to do so. Big pharmaceutical companies fought fiercely increasing HIV-AIDS generic drug availability and lowering prices until August 2003.[9]

Such realities are not accidental. They are the consequence of turning healthcare into a material good, like a car or vacation package. Free-market capitalism, in which many unregulated private healthcare providers, researchers, and insurers compete for the healthcare market, has transformed U.S. healthcare largely from a public service provided to all into a private commodity purchased by some (individuals, employers, limited government programs for the needy).

In terms of the fruits of technological and genetic research on the horizon (e.g., embryonic stem cell research), there is no guarantee that new treatments will become universally available. If capitalism's free-market model predominates, access to these innovations may very well be based upon the ability to pay. Moreover, we may continue to pour millions into research on new drugs that benefit relatively few people (e.g., those with insomnia, restless legs, erectile dysfunction) rather than focus resources on the millions who die from tuberculosis, diabetes, and malaria every year—all highly preventable and treatable diseases. "About half of all global health research and development in recent years was undertaken by private industry, with less than 5 percent going to diseases specific to poor countries. . . . Sixty percent of all profits from international pharmaceutical sales are made in the United States, whereas Africa represents only 1 percent of worldwide sales."[10] Thinking about our global neighbors, what do we need more—new drugs for lethargic libidos or new antibiotics to combat multidrug-resistant tuberculosis?

Catholic ethicist Lisa Cahill asks a similar question: "Does it serve the common good . . . to provide new genetic treatments for the privileged, while so many go uninsured?"[11] We cannot take for granted that for-profit medical research will focus on the most pressing public health needs or that its discoveries and innovations will benefit all equally. Apart from the question of whether using embryos in research is ethical, we also need to address the thorny question of how much funding (public and private) to allot to stem cell and other genetic research versus creating a comprehensive healthcare infrastructure. Spending on the latter would mean millions more people would receive better preventive, diagnostic, and prenatal care in the very near future, while stem cell and genetic therapies to treat Parkinson's, Alzheimer's, spinal cord injuries, and so on may take much longer to develop and may benefit a far fewer number of people overall.

REDEFINING MATTERS OF LIFE AND DEATH: CHRISTIAN CONTRIBUTIONS TO U.S. HEALTHCARE

Religious communities possess distinctive language that can expand society's moral imagination. In fact, many denominations have helpful social statements on healthcare and other topics in medical ethics. Here are three contributions.

Neighbor-Love in Response to Individualism and Healthcare Inequities

For centuries Christians have asked: "Who is our neighbor? What do we owe our neighbor?" Roman Catholics regularly ask what promotes the "common good." When Jesus tells the parable of the Good Samaritan (Luke 10:25–37), he confronts us with the fact that strangers, people from unfamiliar places, non-Christians, and those we do not know personally *are all our neighbors*—sisters and brothers—and that we are accountable for their well-being. "How does God's love abide in anyone who has the world's goods and sees a brother or sister in need and yet refuses help?" (1 John 3:17). In this spirit, people of faith have a moral responsibility to push our elected leaders to enact comprehensive healthcare for all. After all, throughout Scriptures God and Jesus are spoken of as "healer" (e.g., Exod. 15:26; Isa. 25:7–8; Mal. 4:2; Matt. 4:23–25). So as followers of Christ, can we do any less?

To reform healthcare, a powerful myth must be exposed. Many Americans claim that government-sponsored healthcare would be too expensive, take away people's choice of provider, create long waits for care, or would never work. In reality, the U.S. *already has* an effective model that works quite well—in which people choose their care providers and which has far less administrative overhead costs (on average 2 percent per year vs. 13–30 percent for private insurers): Medicare.[12] Currently, it covers people over the age of sixty-five and those with chronic disabilities. We could expand Medicare to include children and all adults.

Change will not be easy. Private insurance companies are a powerful lobby. The intricate matrix of providers, insurers, and policies has created a confusing tangle to sort out, yet we are a country that prides itself on innovation—like mapping the human genome. The argument that universal healthcare is too complicated or too costly fails to convince me. It is not beyond American intelligence to figure out, but it will require moral commitment and grit.

Moreover, the language of "neighbor-love" and "common good" presents important critiques of the strong currents of individualism and consumerism in the United States. When an individualistic and consumerist ethos predominates, bioethical deliberations devolve into "Do I as an individual have a right to purchase the treatment, do the research, profit from it, and so on?" That is a simplistic approach to complex moral questions. Some suffer from an entitlement syndrome—assuming that they are entitled to any treatment—no matter the cost or how spending money on it might limit care or research in other areas.

To illustrate, we spend massive resources on elective cosmetic surgery. In 2004, people in the United States "from ages 19–34 had 427,368 botox procedures, 100,793 laser resurfacing treatments . . . and 1,094 face-lifts."[13] Teenage daughters get nose and eye jobs as birthday, Christmas, and graduation gifts.[14] Our society needs to do some soul-searching. Such choices mean that the time and expertise of medical professionals (along with copious medical supplies—syringes, IV equipment, anesthesia, oxygen, saline, gauze, etc.) go to these elective procedures instead of more life-threatening needs—here and abroad. Drawing upon "neighbor-love" and the "common good" for moral insight could offer a refreshing "reality check" on such "extreme makeovers."

Self-Reflection and Confession in Response to Societal Egoism

Creating comprehensive health coverage for all is a fundamental piece of healthcare reform. However, it is not the only change needed. In addition, we must create structures and practices that help people see, understand, and appreciate those who differ from themselves. Often, we fail in our compassion for our neighbors because we fail to see them as complex, precious children of God.

Jesus warns against being so preoccupied with pointing out others' shortcomings that we forget to look critically at our own (Matt. 7:1–4). When we become self-righteous, we judge others harshly and fail to see the whole person and situation in front of us: Those without insurance are assumed to be here illegally. People who need public assistance are criminals, drug addicts, irresponsible, or lazy. And when healthcare providers see patients primarily through the lens of their disease, insurance status, or assumptions based on racial-ethnic or class background, it diminishes the quality of the care patients receive. Such assumptions are not only ill-conceived, but they also undermine respect for human dignity and diminish society's responses to complicated social problems.

Christianity possesses a rich tradition of confession. People of faith can call for confession of our collective sin of ignoring and discounting our neighbors in need. We can advocate for nuanced attention to (and education about) racial-ethnic, socioeconomic, linguistic, cultural, and religious particularities that shape patient needs, perceptions, experiences of health and illness, and fears. And we must strive to appreciate the complexity of one another's lives *as well as* open ourselves to self-critical reflection. Such self-reflection involves exploring relevant socioeconomic contexts along with our own internal assumptions, privilege, and biases.

We must boldly confess that we have not yet created a society in which all persons have equal opportunity. Racial-ethnic minorities are greatly underrepresented in the health professions. Latinos represent 15 percent and blacks represent 13 percent of the total U.S. population, yet Latinos "make up 2 percent of registered nurses, 3.4 percent of psychologists, and 3.5 percent of physicians . . . and while one in 8 Americans is black, fewer than 1 in 20 physicians or dentists is black."[15] In September 2004, the Sullivan Commission report found that blacks, Native Americans, and Hispanics only compose "nine percent of the nation's nurses, six percent of doctors and five percent of dentists."[16]

Why does this discrepancy matter? Some studies have found that race concordance between patients and doctors contributes to trust and patient satisfaction. Even more, increased leadership of darker-skinned people in healthcare could help transform the cultures and assumptions of medical institutions. Providers of color may propose key changes for how various religious traditions are accommodated, how language translation services are provided, and how a hospital connects with its surrounding neighborhoods through education and prevention programs. People of faith can actively promote healthcare cultures that value self-critical reflection and diversity.

Acknowledging Dependence in Response to Human Mortality and Imperfection

Part of living well means preparing for a good death—one in which pain and fear are minimized and the company and love of family and friends are in great supply. When we resist death at all costs, when we view it as the ultimate foe to defeat and we see life as the absolute good, we verge on turning life into an idol. As Christians, we are called to profess that union with God is the ultimate purpose of human life. Life in itself is not an absolute end.

Christians have an obligation to question our society's inclination to deny human mortality. A fine line exists between the amelioration of human suffering or increasing the quality of life and trying to perfect ourselves—our faces, bodies, children—or to beat death. The Bible and Christianity's greatest prophets and theologians proclaim our radical dependence on God and our inability to become perfect or immortal. This conviction can balance our society's tendency to put so much faith (I use that word intentionally) in technological innovation.

U.S. inhabitants spend a disproportionate amount of money on healthcare in the last six months of life on treatments that often have little therapeutic value. Respecting life does not mean desperately clinging to it, no matter the quality or cost. Hospice programs are far underutilized; yet when hospice is a part of the care plan, patients are less likely to seek means to hasten their deaths because their pain is well-managed and they have the emotional, social, psychological, and spiritual support they need.

When we ponder when or if to use technological measures to save life, the complicated truth is that the same technology—ventilators, nutrition, hydration, and so on—is often basic or morally obligatory treatment in some cases (e.g., right after a car accident when the full scope of injuries is not yet known) yet extraordinary or excessive in others (e.g., in the cases of brain death, massive stroke or heart attack resulting in multiple organ system failure, persistent vegetative state, or end stages of terminal cancer). Blanket rules are not as helpful in discerning the moral path as are honest and thorough discussions with a gathering of the patient, loved ones, skilled and dedicated healthcare providers, and emotional/spiritual caregivers—who are all committed to finding the best outcome for the particular patient in a particular moment.

CONCLUDING PROVOCATIONS

When the subject of dying surfaces in public debate, many zero in on Oregon, the only state where physician-assisted suicide is legal,[17] and too often the range of questions is narrowly confined to assessing the (im)morality of a given action (e.g., pulling the plug, disconnecting the feeding tube, administering lethal doses of medications to terminally ill patients). Such questions matter, and we must continue to explore and pray about them in our families, congregations, care settings, and society. Yet they are not the only questions that need asking.

A pivotal ethical question for end-of-life care—as in all areas of medical ethics and bioethics—is, which lives are most likely to be mistreated or ignored and how can we care for them? Being poor or uninsured and living with a chronic or terminal illness is devastating in this country. People often do not have good—or *any*—options in terms of the providers, care facility, or social and emotional support offered to them. Too many die alone—in unheated apartments, warehoused in dingy nursing homes, under bridges, in alleys. As Christians, what are we committed to do for them?

Abortion, euthanasia, and physician-assisted suicide are not the only pressing life-and-death moral issues. There are millions of vulnerable lives outside the womb or hospital bed whose rights to life are not adequately safeguarded—orphans; foster children; impoverished children, parents, and single adults; the uninsured; survivors of domestic and/or childhood abuse; people suffering from chronic and multigenerational drug and alcohol addiction, to name a few. If we, as a society and as Christians, place a high premium on human life, then we owe much to the lives affected by these social, economic, medical, public health, and political realities.

We need to ask ourselves some hard questions: Do we support safety-net programs: Headstart, food stamps, affordable housing, special education, and day-care programs for children and elders in need? How do we support pregnant teenagers in crisis? Do we dismiss the needs of impoverished single mothers because we judge them as immoral? Do we lobby for excellent public schools and decent salaries for teachers in inner-city neighborhoods? What are we willing to do to make sure everyone has access to adequate and affordable healthcare? In short, how do we create a society—with adequate socioeconomic structures—that is conducive to the well-being and flourishing of all human beings, regardless of race, ethnicity, religion, gender, or socioeconomic status? Is such a bold task part of our vision as Christians for an ethic of life?

U.S. healthcare inadequacies and inequalities make a moral claim upon people of faith. Brazilian theologian Ivone Gebara writes, "We have no consistent record of humanity's progressing in virtues and moral values. Instead we have the impression that at each moment of our history, we have to learn all over again the meaning of giving and receiving respect."[18] It seems to me that our moment in U.S. history calls Christians to advocate earnestly for comprehensive healthcare reform. To discover anew what respect and love mean in healthcare is not simply an intellectual assent; rather, a conversion of the heart is required—a conversion to the love of neighbor and to the common good—and it is precisely here that humble, tenacious, compassionate, hope-filled people of faith can play a vibrant and vital role.

QUESTIONS FOR DISCUSSION

1. Does Linda Miller's story remind you of someone you know? Discuss your experiences with insurance, being under- or uninsured, preexisting conditions, and so on. Brainstorm what you can do to support people in your community who need healthcare.
2. When seeking care, what helps you trust your doctor, nurse, or hospital? Have your encounters with healthcare providers been mostly positive, negative, or fairly mixed? Have you noticed any stereotypes at work? Discuss what can be done to ensure that all people feel heard and respected when they go for medical care.
3. If your denomination has made public statements on healthcare reform, read and discuss them together in your congregation. How might they help guide your public voice and advocacy?
4. What current proposals or models for healthcare reform most intrigue you? What organizations in your community are involved in healthcare reform? What can you learn from them, and how might you support their work?

RESOURCES

Books

Farmer, Paul. *Pathologies of Power: Health, Human Rights, and the New War on the Poor.* Berkeley: University of California Press, 2005.

Vigen, Aana Marie. *Women, Ethics, and Inequality in U.S. Healthcare: "To Count Among the Living."* New York: Palgrave Macmillan, 2006.

Washington, Harriet A. *Medical Apartheid: The Dark History of Medical Experimentation on Black Americans from Colonial Times to the Present.* New York: Doubleday, 2006.

Web Sites

The International Association for Hospice and Palliative Care, www.hospicecare.com.
Physicians for a National Health Program, www.pnhp.org.

NOTES

1. Dotson Rader, "Can You Pay for Your Health Care?" *Parade*, August 15, 2004, 6.
2. See http://www.familiesusa.org/assets/pdfs/map-uninsured-now-exceeds-cum-pol-of-24-states-plus.pdf (accessed September 1, 2007).
3. See http://www.kff.org/uninsured/upload/Myths-about-the-Uninsured-Fact-Sheet.pdf (accessed August 30, 2007).
4. Cathy Schoen, "Insured but Not Protected: How Many Adults Are Underinsured?" *Health Affairs* Web Exclusive, June 14, 2005; available at http://content.healthaffairs.org/cgi/content/abstract/hlthaff.w5.289 (accessed August 15, 2007).
5. Judy Peres, "Breast Cancer Kills More Blacks Than Whites Here: Task Force Formed to See Why Chicago Has Wide Disparity," *Chicago Tribune*, October 18, 2006.
6. Brian D. Smedley et al., eds. *Unequal Treatment: Confronting Racial and Ethnic Disparities in Healthcare*. Washington, DC: National Academies Press, 2003.
7. See http://www.kaisernetwork.org/daily_reports/rep_index.cfm?hint=1&DR_ID=29556, and http://www.kaisernetwork.org/daily_reports/rep_index.cfm?hint=1&DR_ID=30053, http://www.kaisernetwork.org/daily_reports/rep_index.cfm?hint=1&DR_ID=30275 (all accessed May 30, 2005).
8. Jamie Doran, "New York's HIV Experiment," BBC News, November 2004.
9. Lisa S. Cahill, *Theological Bioethics: Participation, Justice, Change* (Washington, DC: Georgetown University Press, 2005), 220.
10. Ibid., 248–49.
11. Ibid., 215.
12. Donald L. Barlett and James B. Steele, *Critical Condition* (New York: Doubleday, 2004), 238.
13. Mary Tannen, "Botox Babies," *The New York Times*, August 28, 2005.
14. Natasha Singer, "For You, My Lovely, A Face-Lift," *The New York Times*, December 29, 2005.
15. Associated Press, "Report Urges Diversity in Health Jobs," February 5, 2004, which references the IOM report, *In the Nation's Compelling Interest: Ensuring Diversity in the Health Care Workforce* (2004).
16. The Sullivan Commission on Diversity in the Healthcare Workforce, *Missing Persons: Minorities in the Health Professions* (Washington, DC: Sullivan Commission, September 2004), 2. Accessible at http://www.aacn.nche.edu/Media/pdf/SullivanReport.pdf.
17. Since 1997, 292 people have died using Oregon's "Death with Dignity Act"; see http://www.oregon.gov/DHS/ph/pas/docs/year9.pdf.
18. Ivone Gebara, *Out of the Depths* (Minneapolis: Fortress, 2002), 96.

Chapter 7

For Financial Security in All Stages of Life

JOHNNY B. HILL

Social Security, once considered a staple in the public policy landscape, is now under assault. Academics, political figures, and journalists alike have argued that the United States cannot afford Social Security for the next generation of retirees. Their grim predictions are often accompanied by proposals to privatize Social Security or to create private personal accounts that would supplement rather than replace the current system. The privatization of Social Security threatens to leave people who are dependent on the system at great risk of being vulnerable to the often unpredictable fluctuations of the market.

What is so striking about debates concerning Social Security is the ambivalent, sometimes even hostile, response of the Christian community to working for creative ways to make Social Security more stable. For instance, right-wing conservative Christian groups, such as Focus on the Family, have been quite adamant in their position that the way to heal society's woes is not through Social Security, but by strengthening marriages and families. These groups ignore the ways in which economic problems wreak havoc on family life and communities. Providing a safety net for all people, particularly the most vulnerable in society, is a key component of Christian community. Christian teachings and practices witness to the concern that Christians should show about proposals to privatize Social Security. What is the relationship of Christian beliefs and practices to public policies concerning Social Security? What types of public policies would be consistent with Christian theological commitments?

ORIGINS OF SOCIAL SECURITY

The intent and origin of Social Security are often lost in proposals for privatization in public debate. As we discuss this debate, we should keep in mind the many programs Social Security offers and why they were created.

Social Security is a way of protecting individuals, families, communities, and businesses from rapidly changing powerful economic and political forces that are common in all areas of our lives. At present, Social Security operates as a pay-as-you-go system where individual taxpayers contribute, based upon their income, to a financial system that manages accounts. However, a taxable wage limit is set, which means that a smaller percentage of the highest paid worker's salaries are taxed to provide for Social Security. In 2007, the taxable wage limit was $97,500. Social security programs generally refer not only to retirement, but also to disability accounts, the Medicare and Medicaid programs, government assistance for low- to no-income persons, and federal housing programs.

Social Security was created in response to problems caused by the lack of governmental regulations of industry in the early twentieth century and the devastating impact of the Great Depression on the lives of all Americans. Few regulations existed at that time to protect workers and provide for their needs throughout all stages of life, even when they could no longer labor in factory, mill, or mine. Working-class people were often not paid enough to satisfy their own basic needs, and in urban areas they were forced to live in unsafe, unsanitary conditions. By 1934, 17 percent of whites and 38 percent of blacks were considered unable to support themselves in any occupation.[1] During this time, nearly 65 percent of African Americans were in need of public assistance, and in places such as Norfolk, Virginia, the numbers rose to a staggering 80 percent in need of public relief.[2]

Many Christians saw it as their moral responsibility to advocate for progressive public policies that would address the needs of the working class and others living in poverty. Social gospelers such as Walter Rauschenbusch, Vida Dutton Scudder, Richard Ely, and Reverdy Ransom critiqued the church for its own complacency in response to the plight of the working poor and used the church's distinctive voice to advocate for change. Among other things, they advocated for an eight-hour workday, security in old age or disability, and laws against child labor. Many of the reforms that they called for later became part of Franklin Delano Roosevelt's New Deal.

Roosevelt signed into law the Social Security Act of 1935 as part of the New Deal; its goal was to provide comprehensive federal "social insurance" protections for workers. Amid the stock market crash of 1929 and the dramatic economic distress and dislocation wrought by the Great Depression, there was a blatant recognition that something had to be done at the federal level to protect workers from the dangerous instability of industrial market forces. Roosevelt's New Deal was a fundamental affirmation that the common good was deeply intertwined with some modest economic security afforded to all Americans. In his 1932 nomination acceptance speech, Roosevelt acknowledged, "This nation is not merely a nation of independence, but it is, if we are to survive, a nation of interdependence."[3] For decades, Social Security has helped to subsidize inadequate pensions of many workers and to provide an income for workers who had been disabled.

PRESERVING SOCIAL SECURITY FOR FUTURE GENERATIONS: A CHRISTIAN CONCERN

A very popular assumption is that individuals today are somehow more capable of managing their own retirements and health insurance. This assumption has supported proposals for the government to disengage from a government-managed Social Security system. Some who question the system fear that the Social Security system will go into bankruptcy before they have a chance to benefit from it themselves. The pervasive trend to pursue a radical retreat from any form of socially responsible governmental policies is most disturbing. This perspective often presupposes the idea that individuals are being paid a living wage with proper benefits that will support a reasonable retirement and health insurance plan. It ignores the reality that many working Americans are living either just above or below the poverty line.

These facts are even more striking among African American, Latino, and Native American communities. Large populations of Americans from diverse backgrounds, including whites, are beholden to some minimal social insurance for survival. Janet Witt, a manager with the National Committee to Preserve Medicare and Social Security, provides a powerful summary when she writes:

> Social Security is the foundation of women's retirement security. Social Security provides 90 percent or more of the total income for 44 percent of all non-married women over 65, 74 percent of non-married African-American women over 65, and 66 percent of non-married Latinas over 65. Social Security prevents massive poverty among the elderly. Without Social Security, over half of all women over 65 and 40 percent of older men would be poor. Social Security also protects 5.4 million children under age 18 who receive part of their family income from Social Security. Social Security also provides lifetime income support to about 750,000 disabled adult children, based on a parent's work record.[4]

Indeed these numbers are staggering. They issue a sobering reminder that Christians and the wider public must act decisively to establish new policy initiatives that will ensure the continuation and enhancement of Social Security programs.

President Bill Clinton announced in his State of the Union Address on January 27, 1998, that there was a critical need for America to reform and "strengthen the Social Security system for the twenty-first century."[5] Although the U.S. Social Security system registers annual revenues of more than $100 billion, the program is dramatically underfunded for future generations.[6] Generations yet unborn will bear the burden of a lack of promised benefits if the problem is not addressed.

But how did we get to this point? How and why have we become so disinterested in building foundations for the future and recognizing the fundamental importance of the common good? Concern for the common good does not negate individual freedom and rights. On the contrary, it is because of a robust concern for the common good that individual human rights are attained and advanced; this type of thinking guided the passing of the Social Security Act in 1935. Christians, in particular, must find creative ways to make the important connection between their beliefs, the values behind them, and the ways in which beliefs interact with the social life. Christians do not exist in isolation. The church is called to live faithfully and responsibly in all areas of life, including allowing faith commitments to inform public policy. Practices such as Communion, worship, forgiveness, justice, reconciliation, and fellowship must guide attitudes and actions toward protecting the sanctity of human life and dignity through Social Security programs.

WHAT DOES COMMUNION HAVE TO DO WITH SOCIAL SECURITY?

In a real sense, Christians of various traditions share an ecumenical theme that centers on the immense theological and ethical significance of Communion in the life of Christian communities. Various Christian communities hold vastly different perspectives on the meaning, content, methods of practice, and overall historical significance of this enduring practice. For instance, the Methodist Church celebrates an open Communion table, described as the Eucharist, where all peoples are welcomed to participate. On the other hand, Eastern Orthodox traditions affirm that only those who are members of their specific community are afforded participation in the Lord's feast. In the Baptist tradition, Communion has come to be described as the Lord's Supper, which sees the elements as symbolic of the actual body and blood of Christ. The Catholic Church understands the practice of Communion as the essential sacrament of the church that brings believers in touch with the actual body and blood of Christ, transcending both time and place, described as transubstantiation. Although practices differ greatly, Christians in all traditions and cultures consider this practice a central part of Christian identity and a primary way of understanding their place in the world. As Christians are invited to share in the Lord's Table, in many ways we are invited to participate in the way and activity of God in Christ in world affairs. Communion is also one of the most challenging mandates of the Christian narrative through its unabashed call to community and radical social concern. The theological meaning of Communion is both comforting and challenging to those of us who desire to live faithfully in accordance with the gospel.

Although the Communion celebration involves a serious personal commitment of relating to God as God relates to individual believers, it is also about community. Communion implies a radical sense of mutual sharing and interrelatedness. Too often in the modern world, Christians have interpreted spiritual practices like Communion as deeply personal and only concerned with individual moral piety. Spiritual practices must be translated into meaningful and transformative social action in the world as well.

Indeed, Communion, as a core symbol of the Christian faith and the church, is personal. However, it is the kind of personal orientation to God that reaches out and longs to express the interrelatedness of God with others. The relationships among those who participate together in Communion are what make faith and God's love meaningful to believers—individually and collectively. Communion should be viewed as an illustration of God's desire for human, social, economic, and political relations. It demonstrates the ways in which God calls believers to community and mutual sharing, and to creation of redemptive social systems that ensure economic security for all.

I believe the members of the early apostolic church of Acts had this in mind as they practiced Communion several times a week. They would also move from house to house, breaking bread together, and "none of them had need."

> They devoted themselves to the apostles' teaching and fellowship, to the breaking of bread and the prayers. Awe came upon everyone, because many wonders and signs were being done by the apostles. All who believed were together and had all things in common; they would sell their possessions and goods and distribute the proceeds to all, as any had need. Day by day, as they spent much time together in the temple, they broke bread at home and ate their food with glad and generous hearts, praising God and having the goodwill of all the people. And day by day the Lord added to their number those who were being saved. (Acts 2:42–47)

In Acts 2 and 4, during the haze of the post-Pentecostal event, the apostles and new followers of Christ were caught in the exuberance of the emerging community of faith coming into being. They certainly believed Jesus' return was imminent. They also maintained that the establishment of the new community of faith was aimed at not only transforming individuals but also redeeming social systems. They were passionate about practicing God's way in the world in a manner that would inspire and transform the existing order.

One of the essential components of this new community was an abiding concern for the spiritual and material condition of every member of the community. All of the needs of the community were met. The thought of some Christians flourishing with lives of extravagant economic prosperity while other Christians live under the demeaning shadows of poverty, unemployment, homelessness, and the like would have been unconscionable. In doing so, their lives became a radical critique to forces of domination, greed, political repression, and exploitation normative of the Hellenistic Roman culture during the time.

But what does Communion have to do with Social Security as a question of public policy? The leap between one of the most fundamental of all Christian practices and the idea of social insurance is seen in our vision of God. Communion is a reminder of the radical self-giving love of God in Jesus Christ, the love that moves in and through Christian believers. The words "Do this in remembrance of me" are not just important as a familiar liturgical refrain; it is a poetic phrase that calls each believer to community, accountability, and love for the other. When Jesus instituted the Lord's Supper, he was establishing a call to spiritual memory that both inspires and renews faith, as well as issuing a call to action and faithfulness. The faithfulness to which we are called, despite the often tempting desire to remain behind ecclesial walls, means living responsibly in all areas of human life. Christians must work indefatigably to help alleviate human suffering often created and exacerbated by rapidly changing market forces that leave many without gainful employment, healthcare, disability insurance, and the prospects for a decent retirement. John Howard Yoder, the esteemed Mennonite scholar and pacifist, made a compelling case for Christian witness in the public sphere when he proclaimed that Christians must live in a way that makes their faith meaningful to the lives of others. By "meaningful," Yoder meant that the church, in particular, must seek to engage issues of human suffering and conflict in peaceful and transformative ways. Although Yoder was often criticized as sectarian for his pacifist commitments, he recognized that for the Christian, there is no distinction between believer and citizen of the state. For Yoder, the Christian life involves seeking to responsibly contribute to the shaping of public policy in a way that reflects the love of God in Christ.

WHY PUBLIC POLICY IS A MATTER OF FAITH

An enduring legacy of the post-Enlightenment perspectives on the Christian life is emphasis on a compartmentalized understanding of who we are as Christians. From this perspective, being Christian has to do with essentially the moral development of the personal autonomous self. Christians, according to this view, have no business engaging in politics or public life in general. The Christian life is personal, pietistic, and above all, concerned with individual moral purity. By taking a closer look at this perspective, we observe how an entire dimension of the Christian life has been policed out of contemporary discourse. We must recover a comprehensive understanding of the Christian life grounded in seeing God as creator. Hence, because God is concerned with all areas of human life, personal and social, public and private, it is critical that Christians express their faith and the values they hold dear in the public square.

The early social movements of the twentieth century attest to the vibrancy and power of Christian witness and its capacity to impact meaningful change in the world. Movements to restrict labor abuses concerning children; campaigns to establish voting rights for women and minority groups; development of public education, utility, and sanitation services; and the like were all informed by the notion that individuals flourish and thrive when there is an abiding concern for the common good. It is very difficult to imagine a world where someone is not dependent in some way on another person for their well-being. Just getting out of bed, pouring our morning cup of coffee, and reading the paper reveals a delicate network of interdependence that inundates our very existence. The shop worker who makes the sheets; the factory worker who packs and ships the coffee; the manager, editors, maintenance workers, and delivery personnel who bring the papers to our doorsteps are all critical to what it means for individuals and groups to live in community together.

THE CURRENT DEBATE: PRAYING AND ADVOCATING

All Christian practices must come into meaningful conversation with the Social Security debate. To deny the reality of unemployment, workplace injuries, and the uncertainties of capitalism's supply/demand system is to permit the continuation of a humanitarian crisis of historic proportions. But for what should people of faith be advocating? What kinds of policies, initiatives, and proposals are we to attend to in our efforts to remain faithful in these times? The notion of privatization continues to guide public debate on these issues; it relates not only to the Social Security retirement program but to all social programs geared toward establishing and maintaining a safety net for American citizens.

While a number of options are being considered to reform the Social Security system, it is critical to support programs that invest in children and families. Although privatization may work in some instances, maintaining a viable and well-funded Social Security system that looks to the future, increasing benefits and resources for those most economically vulnerable, is essential to advancing the common good. Supporters of privatization argue that groups who have typically lacked inheritable wealth would benefit greatly from the establishment of "private pensions."[7] Here, contributions to the payroll tax (known as the Federal Insurance Contribution Act or FICA tax) would go toward private investment accounts that could potentially be passed on to future generations. This approach presupposes a level of private wealth that can sustain individuals and families through periods of unemployment, underemployment, and the unpredictable and dramatic changes of the stock market.[8]

Privatization would be disastrous for millions of Americans. It would lead to wider gaps between rich and poor, and increase the vulnerability of many women and children who rely on Social Security benefits for basic survival. Social Security is more than a retirement plan. It is a way of ensuring family economic stability when a member becomes disabled, divorced, unemployed, retired, or deceased.[9]

J. Gordon Chamberlin, in his book *Upon Whom We Depend: The American Poverty System*, purports that the issue of poverty is a theological issue that lies at the heart of the Christian narrative.[10] For Chamberlin, churches must move beyond rhetoric to action. Simple charity, he says, is merely a way of sustaining the status quo and does little to address the systemic and structural realities of poverty in America. Maintaining Social Security is critical to curtailing the harsh reality of poverty. Preserving and advancing the current Social Security system is not antithetical to the dedicated work of churches in developing creative local and national initiatives to address poverty. However, part of the response must be to insist on solid policies that will nurture and build upon the present Social Security program. The founder and CEO of the Children's Defense Fund, Marian Wright Edelman, offers an illustrative summary: "Efforts to fix the Social Security 'crisis'—by allowing Americans to invest some of their benefits into private accounts—abound. But Social Security, one of the great protections our country offers, has always been meant to be a social insurance policy that guarantees enough, not an investment program that offers a chance for more at the risk of too little."[11]

Robert M. Ball, former commissioner of Social Security from 1962 to 1973 and founding member of the National Academy of Social Insurance, has outlined a seventy-five-year plan that would preserve and enhance the current program. Supported by many progressive Christian communities, Ball's plan calls for the following initiatives:

1. Gradually raise the cap on earnings covered by Social Security so that once again 90 percent of all income would be taxed and counted for benefits.
2. Beginning in 2010, dedicate future proceeds of a revised estate tax to Social Security. Present law gradually reduces the estate tax so that by 2009, only estates above \$3.5 million (\$7 million per couple) will be taxed. The tax should be frozen at that level, with the revenues directed toward Social Security.

3. Improve the return on Social Security funds by investing part of them in equities, as just about all other public and private pension plans do.
4. Adopt the more accurate consumer price index recently developed by the Bureau of Labor Statistics (the so-called chained index) to better account for the substitution of one commodity for another as prices increase.
5. Beginning in 2010, cover all new state and local employees under Social Security. About three-fourths of state and local government employees are already covered. With this extension of coverage, most people who work would be under Social Security.[12]

The essence of Ball's proposal for preserving Social Security has been repeated by Jim Wallis, Jesse Jackson, Bill Clinton, Virginia Reno and Joni Lavery of the National Academy of Social Security, Marian Wright Edelman, and many others. Together, they constitute a mighty chorus of Christians and others from various faith traditions, cultures, and economic groups that make up the American sociopolitical landscape, calling for the perseverance and solvency of Social Security today.

As people of faith, we have a real opportunity to shape policies and legislation in ways that protect, affirm, and sustain human life—programs that value all human flourishing, not just for the elite. The rapidly changing tides of public policy debate demand that Christians support and struggle for policies that help to ease human suffering and promote robust communities of mutual respect and adoration. Of course, there are no guarantees that any specific public policies that citizens attempt to engage will always lead to a desirable response. However, the church remains faithful in its quest to make faith meaningful to the lives of those who are hurting—the hungry, homeless, abused, neglected, wounded, and voiceless among us. In doing so, we are assured of tenacious participation in the work of Jesus Christ in the world.

QUESTIONS FOR DISCUSSION

1. Do Christians have any responsibility to help establish public policies that serve the common good?
2. What is the relationship between the Christian practice of Communion and Social Security?
3. To what extent do social realities like racism, poverty, economic exploitation, and unemployment play a role in the development of social security policies?
4. How might we as Christians engage in meaningful practices that help promote responsible social policies in practical, everyday ways?

RESOURCES

Buto, Kathleen, Martha Priddy Patterson, William E. Spriggs, and Maya Rockeymoore. *Strengthening Community: Social Insurance in a Diverse America.* Washington, DC: Brookings Institution Press, 2004.

Epstein, Abraham. *Insecurity: A Challenge to America*, 2nd rev. ed. New York: Random House, 1938.

Schieber, Sylvester J., and John B. Shoven. *The Real Deal: The History and Future of Social Security*. New Haven, CT: Yale University Press, 1999.

NOTES

1. John Hope Franklin and Alfred A. Moss Jr., *From Slavery to Freedom: A History of African Americans* (New York: McGraw-Hill, 1994), 384.
2. Ibid.
3. Ibid. See Franklin D. Roosevelt, Speech Accepting the Democratic Nomination for President, 1932.
4. Janet Witt, "Social Insurance: Guaranteed Benefit, Life-Long Family Protection," *Church and Society,* May/June 2005, 22–23.
5. President William J. Clinton, State of the Union Address, January 27, 1998, available at http://www.ssa.gov/history/clntstmts.html.
6. Sylvester J. Schieber and John B. Shoven, *The Real Deal: The History and Future of Social Security* (New Haven, CT: Yale University Press, 1999), 1.
7. Maya Rockeymoore, "Social Security Privatization and African-Americans," *Church and Society,* May/June 2005, 70–71.
8. Ibid.
9. Joan Entmacher, "Women and Social Security," *Church and Society,* May/June 2005, 75–81.
10. J. Gordon Chamberlin, *Upon Whom We Depend: The American Poverty System* (New York: Peter Lang, 1999), 127–42.
11. Marian Wright Edelman, "The Social Security Debate: 'Crisis' or Cherished Public Compact?" *Church and Society,* May/June 2005, 95.
12. Robert M. Ball, "Fixing Social Security," *Church and Society,* May/June 2005, 124–25.

Chapter 8

For Immigrants

MIGUEL A. DE LA TORRE

The government's affidavit was dated June 21, 1960. Citing Section 242 of the Immigration and Nationality Act, the letter placed me on notice that deportation procedures were imminent. I was ordered to voluntarily depart from the United States in lieu of forced expatriation. From the moment I received this affidavit until the day I received my naturalization papers in 1969, I was an undocumented immigrant, what some today insist on calling an illegal immigrant. Ironically, I found myself in the country directly responsible for my exile from my homeland, Cuba. My family's presence in this country was a direct result of U.S. foreign policies that deprived Cubans of sovereignty during the first half of the twentieth century. The irony of the present immigration debate, a paradox conveniently ignored by politicians and unknown to many average citizens, is that U.S. policies are directly responsible for the Hispanic presence in this country.

U.S. POLICY IN LATIN AMERICA: A HISTORY TOO OFTEN IGNORED OR FORGOTTEN

Most undocumented immigration occurs by crossing the artificial line created immediately after the U.S. territorial conquest of northern Mexico, ending with the Mexican-American War (1846–1848). From Tijuana on the Pacific Ocean to Matamoros on the Gulf of Mexico runs a 1,833-mile border separating the southwestern United States from the rest of Latin America. Flowing southeastwardly from the midway point on the border at Ciudad Juárez to Matamoros is the Rio Grande, literally the Big River; ironically, the word *grande* (big) is a misnomer. The river is narrow and shallow in several places, allowing for easy crossing. The rest of the border, from Ciudad Juárez toward the west, is little more than a line drawn upon the ground. Parts of this line are demarcated by a fifteen-foot-high wall. Landing strips used during the First Iraq War were recycled in 1994 by the Immigration and Naturalization Service (INS) to construct this wall. The hope of INS was to stem the flow of mainly Mexican immigrants through the San Diego area and Nogales, Arizona, but the flow continues, only now through miles of hazardous deserts where many fall victim to the elements. This artificial line is more than just a border between two countries. Some have called it a scar caused by the first and third worlds rubbing up against each other.

During a September 8, 2002, interview with the *New York Times*, former Secretary of State Colin Powell declared, "Our record and our history is not one of going out looking for conflict. It is not one of undertaking pre-emptive acts for the purpose of seizing another person's territory, or to impose our will on someone else." Powell, along with most U.S. citizens, has created the myth that this country has never invaded another country for territorial gain. Sustaining such an assumption leads to the false conclusion that all Hispanics immigrated to the United States, when in reality, the United States immigrated to lands held by Latino/as.

Most Euro-Americans have forgotten that the United States invaded Mexico to seize another people's territory. The justification of this massive land acquisition was based on a theology referred to as Manifest Destiny, which taught that God intended Euro-Americans to physically take possession of the entire continent. Like the Promised Land given to Israel of old, Euro-Americans, due to their so-called racial superiority, were entrusted by God to tame the wilderness. In 1885, Reverend Josiah Strong captured this sentiment as he wrote that "God, with infinite wisdom and skill, is training the Anglo-Saxon race for an hour sure to come in the world's future. . . . If I read not amiss, this powerful race will move down upon Mexico, down upon Central and South America, out upon the islands of the sea, over upon Africa and beyond. And can any one doubt that the result of this competition of races will be the 'survival of the fittest'?"[1]

The expansionist war against Mexico was seen as the primary step toward achieving Manifest Destiny. In July 1845, General Zachary Taylor encroached on Mexican territory by deploying his troops to bait the Mexicans. Once Mexico mobilized to meet its adversary, President Polk (who was elected on his support of the annexation of Texas and the war with Mexico) had the opportunity to request a declaration of war from Congress. A military onslaught by the puissant North led to Mexico's capitulation and to the 1848 Treaty of Guadalupe-Hidalgo, which ceded half of Mexico's territory to the United States. This land included gold deposits that would be discovered in California in 1849, silver deposits in Nevada, oil in Texas, and all of the natural harbors (except Veracruz) necessary for commerce, hence enriching the United States while depriving Mexico's future ability to create wealth.

To make matters worse, the treaty agreements and historic land titles after the war were ignored by the U.S. government, hence providing "legal" means of seizing lands owned by Mexicans. Mexican Americans were reduced to a "reserve army" of laborers, allowing the overall southwestern economy to develop at their expense. Out of necessity, Mexican Americans worked at the lowest wage level in the mining and agriculture industries, thereby consolidating the power and wealth of the Euro-Americans. The luxurious houses of Los Angeles, San Antonio, and Santa Fe were built at considerable cost as to distance their privileged space from the menace of *el barrio*. The U.S. expansionist war to seize land and make this development for Euro-Americans possible has been conveniently forgotten by our political leaders and many others.

WHY DO THEY KEEP COMING?

Many were already here; it was the borders that crossed them. Others traveled north, crossing the border created through U.S. military power. But why did they come? Why do they continue to come? "They come to take away jobs and use up social services created for real Americans." "They come in search of the American Dream hoping to find a better life for themselves and their families." These are the two most common answers given. Both answers are wrong. The real reason "they" keep coming is bananas, and our refusal to deal with the role of bananas contributes to much of the misinformation surrounding the current immigration debate.

Before 1870, most Americans had never heard of bananas. Two individuals, Lorenzo Dow Baker and Minor Keith, are credited with being the first to introduce bananas to the American consumer. By 1880, Baker and Keith, along with Andrew Preston, a Boston entrepreneur, joined forces to create the Boston Fruit Company. By 1899, Americans were consuming over 16 million bunches of bananas a year. That was also the year that Boston Fruit merged with United Fruit to create the notorious United Fruit Company, the largest banana company in the world, with plantations throughout Central America, South America, and the Caribbean.

Obviously the problem is not with the bananas themselves, but with what they symbolize. Bananas, or more directly, the pursuit of wealth by Euro-Americans by using the natural resources of Latin American nations, could only be accomplished with the full might of the U.S. armed forces. Around this time President Theodore Roosevelt started talking about "gunboat diplomacy" and "speaking softly but carrying a big stick." While most of us remember these sayings from grade school, few truly understand their impact on the histories of Central and South America. Roosevelt was describing how the full force of the U.S. military was at the disposal of U.S. corporations, such as the United Fruit Company, to protect their interests.

Let's use Guatemala as an example of how U.S. foreign policy and U.S. business interests worked together to create the present immigration situation. When Manuel Estrada Cabrera, the Guatemalan dictator, gave the United Fruit Company free rein to own land so the company could grow bananas in 1901, the U.S. military made sure that United Fruit Company's interests were well protected. Not only was Guatemala under the control of U.S. companies—hence the term "banana republic"—but so was almost every nation along the Caribbean Sea (along with several South American countries). The sovereignty of most Latin American countries was undermined because they needed the expressed blessings of the U.S. ambassador before choosing their leaders.

By the 1950s, 70 percent of the land in Guatemala was controlled by 2.2 percent of the population, with only 10 percent of the land available to 90 percent of the mostly indigenous population. Guatemala's predicament was the established norm throughout most of Latin America. Most of the land was unused, and owned by large landowners. Jacobo Arbenz was eventually elected president through a free and open election. He implemented land reforms to deal with this injustice. However, he ran into one insurmountable problem: the United Fruit Company was a major holder of unused land. To protect their interest, the U.S. government overthrew the democratically elected government of Guatemala and replaced it with a military dictatorship under the pretense that Arbenz was a communist. Of course, Guatemala is not the only country where the United States installed brutal dictators who would protect the business interests of U.S. corporations. Almost every country along the Caribbean has been invaded by the United States at least once during the twentieth century.[2]

The result of U.S.-installed banana republics created poverty, strife, and death in all of these countries. Inevitably, resistance to the United States manifested itself as fight or flight. Hundreds of thousands were killed or disappeared, while millions fled north. Many are Central Americans, especially from Guatemala, El Salvador, and Nicaragua, who settled in urban areas including New York City, Los Angeles, and Washington, D.C. Those from El Salvador and Nicaragua immigrated because of U.S. wars conducted in their country either by supporting the oppressive regime (as in the case of El Salvador), or by funding the rebel forces (as in the case of Nicaragua). The inability to contain military violence to just one nation would contribute to migration in the surrounding countries affected by the war.

Violence need not simply be physical to cause migration; it can also be economic violence, as demonstrated by the *maquiladora* industry along the U.S.-Mexican border. The passage of the 1994 North American Free Trade Agreement (NAFTA) helped anchor Mexico's economy on the thirty-five hundred foreign-owned factories along its border by lowering trade barriers with the United States and Canada. These U.S. corporations straddling the border exist so that U.S. companies can export component parts and machinery duty-free to Mexico. Upon reentering the United States, rather than being taxed upon the full value, tariffs are only levied upon the value added to the component by the cheap labor process. Unfortunately, corporate profits are created at the expense of Mexican workers. Real income for Mexican wage earners lost 20 percent of its purchasing power since NAFTA spurred the growth of *maquiladoras*, even though wages and benefits for *maquiladora* employees rose by 86 percent from 1997 to 2002 to an average of $6,490 a year. But a rise in wages is deceptive when we consider that the national minimum wage fell by nearly 50 percent in value over the last decade.[3] As conditions worsen, Mexican workers began to raise questions concerning plant safety, living wages, and the environment. U.S. factories are responding by relocating elsewhere—specifically China, where wages are even cheaper. Why then should we be surprised that more and more dissatisfied workers attempt the hazardous border crossing to the north?

This scenario brings us back to the question at hand: why do *they* keep coming? When the U.S. military provided the freedom for U.S. corporations like the United Fruit Company to build roads into these developing countries to extract, by brute force if necessary, their natural resources, and when *maquiladoras* along the border extracted cheap labor, some of the inhabitants of those countries, deprived of a livelihood, took those same roads to follow their resources. They come following what has been stolen from them. They come to escape the violence and terrorism we unleashed upon them. We have an immigration problem because, for more than a century, we have exploited and continue to exploit Latin America.

FALSE ASSUMPTIONS MADE ABOUT UNDOCUMENTED WORKERS

Federal legislators have been wrestling with how to bring about much-needed immigration reform. Unfortunately, the tide of anti-immigration sentiment has negatively impacted legislators' abilities to achieve comprehensive reform. Some of these sentiments have found expression in rhetoric advocated by politicians and radio talk-show hosts who have undermined the national immigration debate. Among the many false assumptions voiced are as follows:

"They are using up our services and contributing nothing financially."

This statement reduces migrants to a formula that determines if they represent a social gain or a social cost to the common good. The worldview this represents ignores their humanity and declares that aliens get to stay if they provide a social gain; if not, they are deported. Even this flawed ethical framework reveals that immigrants should stay; the Bell Policy Center estimates that undocumented immigrants add $10 billion to the U.S. economy annually. They are responsible for building, not fleecing, our economy.[4] The Center for Immigration Studies, a nonpartisan D.C. research institution that favors restrictive immigration policies, admitted that undocumented households create a net benefit of $7 billion annually to Social Security and Medicare programs.[5] Ironically, the undocumented are supporting Social Security and Medicare for the next generation of documented Americans.

"They are taking away our jobs."

This present wave of immigrants coincides with the lowest national unemployment rate and the fastest economic growth since the early 1900s. Ignored is the fact that in 2004, undocumented workers held 6.3 million out of 146 million jobs, or about 4.3 percent of all U.S. jobs. The growth in undocumented immigrant jobs, according to the U.S. Bureau of Labor Statistics, occurred in service occupations and other industries requiring minimal education or skills. In the coming decade, the number of low-skilled jobs is expected to grow by seven hundred thousand per year. Most undocumented immigrant labor tends to be low skilled when compared to native workers and seldom threatens native-born workers' jobs. Hence, undocumented immigrant labor contributes to economic growth while having a minimal impact on unemployment or wages paid to native-born workers. According to the National Research Council, immigration reduced wages of competing native-born workers by 1 to 2 percent.[6]

"They don't want to learn English."

This false assumption has led many states to pass "English-only" laws, yet no one needs to convince immigrants of the importance of learning English. Those in poverty because of their immigrant status are keenly aware that proficiency in English is closely correlated with socioeconomic advancement. The desire to learn English is evident in the fierce competition for the few available seats in English-as-a-second-language (ESL) classes. According to a June 12, 2007, article in the *Wall Street Journal*, three out of four ESL applicants wanting to learn English are turned away in New York City. Yet, while the government is demanding aliens learn English, the Bush administration scaled back funding for ESL classes from $570 million to $207 million for the 2006 fiscal year.

"They increase the rate of crime."

Excessive media coverage of crimes and gang activities have led many to believe that immigrants, specifically Latino/a immigrants, commit crimes at higher rates than native-born Americans. Yet according to the Justice Department, only 6 percent of U.S. prisoners (federal and state) are noncitizens (compared with the 7 percent of the population they represent).[7] For a variety of reasons, the crime rate is actually lower among immigrants (both legal and undocumented) than native-born Americans. Census information, police records, and other sources showed that a large increase of undocumented immigration into an area did not cause a rise in the area's crime rate. Rather, studies show the opposite, that crime was reduced. Harvard sociologist Robert J. Sampson argues that aliens desire to advance; thus they work hard and stay out of trouble.[8] Nevertheless, conservative politicians and radio talk-show hosts have successfully used the politics of fear and manipulation to define ethnic minorities, specifically Hispanics, as an alien "other" that threatens America.

"They are lawbreakers who enter the country illegally."

The assumption is that all immigrants broke the law by crossing the border, but according to the Department of Homeland Security, about 75 percent of today's immigrants have permanent visas. Of the 25 percent who are undocumented, 40 percent overstayed their temporary visas.[9] Why then have the opponents to immigration consistently used the term "illegal" to describe aliens? Stereotyping aliens as lawbreakers, and by extension all Hispanics as lawbreakers, appeals to racism for political gains. Creating fear among the voters—in this case, fear of the Hispanic alien—is an effective tool to bring out the vote in certain swing states. Unfortunately, a more disturbing trend is developing. Since September 11, 2001, a link is being developed between the causes of terrorism within the United States and the undocumented. Yet no security expert has ever said that restrictive immigration measures could have prevented the 9/11 attacks. Remember, the hijackers of that day were in the United States on legal visas. In spite of the myriad measures targeting immigrants in the name of national security, few if any terrorist have been apprehended in relation to immigration.[10]

"They are bringing diseases into the country."

Fear of contagious diseases has effectively been used by nativists to combat immigration for the past century. Fear of the Latino/a immigrant is heightened with stories of them infecting Americans with horrific diseases like tuberculosis, malaria, gonorrhea, syphilis, vicious bed bugs, hepatitis, chagas (*Trypanosoma cruzi*, a parasitic insect that feeds on vital organs), and neurocysticercosis, a brain infection caused by a pork tapeworm. Fabrications of disease-carrying undocumented aliens reach absurd levels, as demonstrated by CNN correspondent Lou Dobbs, who during *Lou Dobbs Tonight* claimed that because of "illegal" immigration, when there once were "nine hundred cases of leprosy for forty years [there are now] seven thousand in the past three years." In spite of Dobbs's assertions that the seven thousand figure in the past three years was probably an underestimation, the federal government numbers show a total of seven thousand cases of leprosy identified over the past thirty years, not three years.[11] In addition, according to the Centers for Disease Control (CDC), there is no evidence to verify this claim. In fact, upon contacting the CDC one learns that this government agency does not believe that the incidence of diseases attributed to the undocumented immigrants is important enough to cover or report.[12]

A CAUSE FOR CHRISTIAN CONCERN AND RESPONSE

These popular attitudes and false assumptions made about immigrants are a cause of serious concern for Christians because the claims are not supported by history or the lived experience of immigrants today, and the biblical text has much to say about welcoming strangers and aliens. The phrase that appears most often in the Bible (after "do not be afraid") is to take care of the "alien within your midst." Throughout the Bible we are reminded of God's concern for the alien and the stranger. Aliens and strangers in the Bible are those who have been victimized, oppressed, or enslaved by others; those who are vulnerable because of lack of family connections or support; and those whose nationality or religion differs from the dominant culture. In the exodus story, God told the Israelites to welcome the stranger because "you were once aliens in the land of Egypt." In Ruth, a Moabite woman "clings to" her mother-in-law Naomi to provide her security in old age even though she could have returned to her own people. The Good Samaritan in Luke does not leave the alien on the side of the road, or build walls to avoid seeing his injuries; he takes social and economic risks to attend to the alien's needs. We are challenged again and again to welcome the alien in our midst.

The call to Christian responsibility toward aliens is so paramount that God incarnated Godself as an alien. The radicalness of the incarnation is not so much that the Creator of the universe became a frail human, but rather that God chose to become an alien, fleeing the oppressive consequences of the empire of the time. In so doing, Jesus willingly assumed the role of the ultra-disenfranchised. Over two thousand years ago the Holy Family arrived in Egypt as political refugees, migrants fleeing the tyrannical regime of Herod. Jesus too was an undocumented alien, a victim of circumstances beyond his comprehension or control. Jesus understands what it means to be seen as inferior because he was from a culture different from the dominant one. I have no doubt that Jesus wept as a child for the same reasons many aliens weep today. Those of us who are or have been undocumented aliens discover a savior who knows our fears and frustrations.

How then do we respond to the alien who is criminalized by the dominant culture? The New Sanctuary Movement is, first and foremost, an interfaith movement designed to enable congregations to publicly provide hospitality and protection to a limited number of undocumented families whose cases reveal the moral contradictions of our present immigration laws. In addition, these congregations are committed to support legislation that brings about reform. Families targeted are those who will be deported even though they have a good working record and have children who are U.S. citizens. Each congregation will offer hospitality for three months, at which time the family rotates to another congregation until its case is resolved. The congregation will not be violating federal law because the family's identity is made public.

In September 2006, Elvira Arellano, a thirty-two-year-old undocumented cleaning woman, walked into a Chicago church and requested the right of sanctuary, an ancient practice of seeking refuge in a sacred place. Her actions were a desperate attempt to avoid separation from her seven-year-old son, Saul, who is a U.S. citizen (she was eventually deported on August 19, 2007). Her act of disobedience sparked this New Sanctuary Movement, creating a possible new path to citizenship for many who are undocumented. Religious congregations throughout the United States are coming together as a response to the injustices faced by the undocumented. Church doors are opening to provide undocumented families with legal assistance, child care, and advice on how to locate missing families.

WHAT IS TO BE DONE?

The past years have witnessed an attempt to come to terms with the presence of undocumented aliens. Not all of these attempts are positive, and many merit an offsetting Christian response.

1. Laws and regulations that criminalize a group of individuals create an environment of racial profiling where overt expressions of ethnic discrimination, specifically toward Latino/as, both immigrants and U.S. citizens, flourish. Christians can work to overcome this immoral situation, where possible

employers and social service agencies, fearing governmental reprisals, find it financially safer to discriminate against those who appear "foreign."

2. Denying preventive healthcare services to any human being based on documented status is inhumane, against the express mandate of the biblical text (i.e., the story of the Good Samaritan), and places an increased burden on emergency health services.

3. Refusing to enforce labor protection based on documentation status hurts all workers, including native-born, by allowing the continuation of labor exploitation. When workers' rights are denied to one group, labor standards are lowered, negatively impacting all workers.

4. Refusing to seriously consider the economic realities of the immigration debate, and responding to it by creating a safe and orderly manner for immigrants to enter the United States, creates a humanitarian crisis where those crossing the border find death in the desert, fall into the hands of unscrupulous human smugglers, or find employment with unprincipled business owners.

5. Breaking up families is cruel and inhumane, causing psychological damage to children separated from their parents. When the well-publicized Swift plant raids occurred on December 12, 2006, arresting thirteen hundred undocumented workers, hundreds of their children, who are U.S. citizens by birth, found themselves without a nurturing parent. Family values cannot solely focus on the family of those privileged by whiteness or class. All have a right to be united with loved ones.

6. The reduction of people to the objectified status of "illegal immigrants" contradicts the *imago Dei* (the image of God) possessed by all humans. This *imago Dei* safeguards basic human rights to (a) a living wage, (b) safety from physical or emotional trauma, and (c) family unity. Our present immigration laws deny these basic human rights to over 12 million undocumented aliens residing in the United States.

CONCLUSION

The call to Christians today is to listen carefully to the biblical witness to provide hospitality and to welcome the stranger. We need to speak clearly and to provide shelter with laws and regulations that do not deny worker rights to any group laboring in our nation. We are called to encourage employers and social service workers not to financially discriminate against undocumented workers or deny healthcare benefits to them. We should refuse to consider any legislation that does not see the immigration debate as a humanitarian crisis and work to maintain family unity, to prevent the senseless deaths of those seeking to immigrate to the United States, and to protect all workers regardless of their status as citizens.

QUESTIONS FOR DISCUSSION

1. Describe the experience of immigrants in your area. How are immigrants portrayed by the media? By politicians? By religious leaders? Are they people to fear? To pity? To welcome? How are your local community and church responding to the plight of immigrants? Is this response biblical? Why or why not?
2. In light of the history of U.S. policies that have helped create the need for people to emigrate from Central and South America to the United States, what responsibility do you think the nation has to provide for and welcome immigrants? What responsibility does the church have? What responsibility do U.S. corporations have? Should businesses that outsource jobs be required to pay wages equivalent to those in the United States? Should we be responsible for paying reparations?
3. List the ways you benefit from the labor of undocumented aliens (i.e., cheaper products, reserve army of cheap labor, etc.). Find biblical passages that provide guidance toward how workers are to be treated. How faithful are you and your church to these biblical mandates?
4. Elvira Arellano was recently separated from her son and deported. Did the U.S. government act justly? What responsibilities does your church and your community have toward Ms. Arellano? To her son? Has your church or community done anything? If so, what? If not, what can it do?

RESOURCES

Books

De La Torre, Miguel. *Doing Christian Ethics from the Margins.* Maryknoll, NY: Orbis Books, 2004.

Interfaith Worker Justice, eds. *For You Were Once a Stranger.* Chicago: Interfaith Worker Justice, 2007.

Wilbanks, Dana W. *Re-Creating America: The Ethics of U.S. Immigration and Refugee Policy in a Christian Perspective.* Nashville: Abingdon Press, 1996.

Web Sites

Bell Policy Center, www.thebell.org.

Don't Blame Immigrants for Terrorism, www.cato.org/dailys/10-23-01.html.

Immigration and Naturalization, www.ncjrs.org/ondcppubs/publications/enforce/border/ins_3.html.

National Hispanic Christian Leadership Conference, www.nhclc.org.

National Research Council, www.sites.nationalacademies.org/nrc/index.htm.

The New Sanctuary Movement, www.newsanctuarymovement.org.

No More Deaths, www.nomoredeaths.org.

NOTES

1. Robert F. Smith. *What Happened in Cuba? A Documentary History* (New York: Twayne), 85–87.
2. During the twentieth century either U.S. military incursions or covert/indirect operations (**bold**) occurred in the following countries so as to bring about regime change or protect status quo: Cuba, 1906, 1912, 1917, 1933, **1960**, **1961**; Costa Rica, **1948**; Dominican Republic, **1904**, 1916–24, **1930**, **1963**, 1965; El Salvador, **1932**, **1944**, **1960**, **1980**, **1984**; Granada, 1983; Guatemala, **1921**, **1954**, 1960, **1963**, **1966**; Haiti, **1915**, 1994; Honduras, 1905, 1907, **1911**, **1943**, **1980**; Mexico, 1905, 1914, 1917; Nicaragua, **1909**, 1910, 1912, 1926, **1934**, **1980**, **1981**, **1983**, **1984**; Panama, 1908, 1918, 1925, **1941**, **1981**, 1984.
3. David Bacon, "World Labor Needs Independence and Solidarity," *Monthly Review* 52, no. 3 (July/August 2000): 84–102.
4. National Research Council, "The New Americans: Economic, Demographic, and Fiscal Effect of Immigration" (Washington, DC: National Academies Press, 1997), 6.
5. Center for Immigration Studies, "The High Cost of Cheap Labor: Illegal Immigration and the Federal Budget-Executive Summary." See www.cis.org/articles/2004/fiscalexec.html.
6. Rich Jones, Wade Buchanan, Robin Baker, and Daniel Spivey, "Immigration Effects on Colorado and the Nation: A Review of Research," ed. Heather McGregor (Denver: The Bell Policy Center), 4.
7. Paige M. Harrison and Allen J. Beck, "Prison and Jail Inmates at Midyear 2005," Bureau of Justice Statistics, U.S. Department of Justice, May 2006, 1.
8. "Open Doors Don't Invite Criminals: Is Increased Immigration Behind the Drop in Crime?" *New York Times*, March 11, 2006.
9. Department of Homeland Security (http://uscis.gov/graphics/shared/statistics/index.htm).
10. Associated Press, "U.S. Senate Subcommittee Hears Immigration Testimony," Oct. 17, 2001. According to my knowledge, Zacarias Moussaoui, the "twentieth hijacker" of 9/11, is the only example of a terrorist who was arrested on an immigration violation before the 9/11 attack. Moussaoui, however, was not one of the hijackers on the plane but has been accused of planning to be.
11. David Leonhardt, "Truth, Fiction and Lou Dobbs," *New York Times*, May 30, 2007.
12. See www.cdc.gov.

Chapter 9

For People Lacking Affordable Housing

ROSETTA E. ROSS

How do persons develop as healthy, productive citizens across our country? Is consistent access to secure, affordable, sufficient housing among the priorities necessary for such development? Habitat for Humanity CEO Jonathan Reckford notes that the quality of housing stabilizes families, individuals, and communities. Housing, Reckford says, "can also be a catalyst for social and democratic development." In addition to their importance for societal and individual adult development, stable living environments are especially important to giving children a healthy start. "Children of home owners are more likely to graduate from high school and college and have higher math and reading scores, fewer behavioral problems, and fewer alcohol and substance abuse problems than do children of renters. They are also less likely to become pregnant as teenagers."[1] For adults, housing stability makes finding and keeping work less difficult because contact with employers by mail or telephone and the ability to keep regular work hours increase when shelter is consistent. Whether homes are rented or owned, the emotional well-being provided through stability, security, and sufficiency are essential to a healthy start for children and for supporting all adults.

Although many persons take for granted the meaning of "access to," "secure," "affordable," and "sufficient" housing, clarifying usage of these terms may help answer questions about the importance of housing to developing healthy, productive citizens. Housing "access" means the ability to freely occupy and use a dwelling for shelter. Housing access occurs through renting, home ownership, and various allowances of free occupation. "Secure" housing means lodging that is relatively free from dangers, fears, anxieties, and losses that may be attached to one's living conditions. Security consists in freedom from regular break-ins, physical harm, exposure to the elements, and the like. As defined by the U.S. Department of Housing and Urban Development (HUD), "affordable" housing is available when no more than 30 percent of household income is required to pay for housing. When families pay more than 30 percent of their income for housing, affording other necessities becomes difficult. HUD reports that an

> estimated 12 million renter and homeowner households now pay more than 50 percent of their annual incomes for housing, and a family with one full-time worker earning the minimum wage cannot afford the local fair-market rent for a two-bedroom apartment anywhere in the United States. The lack of affordable housing is a significant hardship for low-income households preventing them from meeting their other basic needs, such as nutrition and healthcare, or saving for the future of their families.[2]

For some families, finding affordable housing has meant sacrificing the quality of housing they inhabit. "Sufficient" housing relates to the quality of a dwelling. "Sufficient housing" is enough to meet a family's needs and is in a condition that does not compromise the health or emotional security of its inhabitants, which includes not being overcrowded. Families with lower incomes often must sacrifice housing sufficiency for affordability by sharing with relatives or other families to reduce housing costs. In Thurmond, California, where migrant farm workers make about twelve thousand dollars annually, families share makeshift trailers with other families because prices to rent apartments in adjacent residential areas easily exceed two thousand dollars per month. If consistently secure, affordable, sufficient housing is among the priorities necessary for developing healthy productive citizens, how do we ensure its accessibility and availability?

ACCESS TO HOUSING IN U.S. HISTORY

Historically, there was a generalized presumption in the United States that all "citizens" would have consistent access to some level of secure, affordable, sufficient housing. Unfortunately, not all persons were full citizens. At times, white women could not own property and depended on access to secure housing through their roles as wives, mothers, daughters, and sisters of propertied white men. In the early years of the United States, Native Americans were forcibly removed from their traditional lands and patterns of living and onto reservations with inadequate living conditions. During the colonial era when 95 percent of the population lived in rural areas, housing was directly related to one's land access and what could be built independently (and in some communities collectively). Many persons built their own shelter. For the overwhelming majority of African Americans, of course, the status of being enslaved meant that they were not citizens and not entitled to normal housing access. Most enslaved persons lived in slave pens. After Emancipation, most formerly enslaved persons were left without adequate local, state, or federal support to determine housing and employment options for themselves. In the South, a system of sharecropping—wherein black persons traded labor for shares of crops, goods, meager wages, and piecemeal shacks—replaced enslavement and continued until the mid-twentieth century.

As cities emerged across the United States, working poor families often have not had the same access to everything presumed to belong to citizens. During the Industrial Revolution, many newly rich industrialists built splendid mansions. Most workers, on the other hand—including working-class European Americans as well as African Americans who migrated to cities to escape sharecropping—lived in small, constricted houses near open sewers and in overcrowded neighborhoods. Coupled with long, sometimes dangerous working conditions, lack of hygienic living circumstances meant that many persons died of disease. Housing discrimination based on race, ethnicity, and national origin restricted housing access for some persons. African Americans and so-called ethnic Europeans, such as Polish, Irish, and Jewish immigrants, were placed in even more challenging living contexts.

When regulations relating to working conditions and housing standards developed, living conditions improved for many industrial workers. Race was a particularly significant marker of housing access near the end of the nineteenth and well into the twentieth centuries. The 1882 Chinese Exclusion Act and the 1943–46 internment of people of Japanese descent prevented or disrupted these Americans' normal housing access. Many Japanese Americans never recovered homes or possessions they left behind when they were interned. Between 1890 and 1930, violence became a regular practice to ensure residential segregation in towns and in subsections of cities from California to Florida.[3] Race discrimination in housing persisted beyond the mid-twentieth century through bank redlining—the practice of excluding communities by failing to grant mortgages or charging excessive rates for mortgages—in black neighborhoods.

In more recent times, mental health policy, cuts in government support, poverty, racial/ethnic identity, and disasters continue to determine whether or not persons have regular access to secure, affordable, sufficient housing. In 1963, the U.S. Community Mental Health Act effected release of several hundred thousand persons from state mental facilities. Although it originally was promoted as community care and related to patients' rights, the Community

Mental Health Act eventually increased the number of homeless persons since deinstitutionalization left the former patients without sufficient support to help them care for themselves. Today, mental health challenges account for about 16 percent of persons who are homeless.[4]

During the 1980s, budget cuts of federal housing subsidies cut in half the number of low-cost rental units (sharply contrasting with the 1970s), while low-income rental households increased. Urban areas felt deeply the loss of quality family housing, and steep increases in the number of homeless persons were a result.[5] The concentration of people of color in urban areas meant these communities experienced the loss most intensely. For example, African Americans, who represent about 14 percent of the U.S. population, are 49 percent of the homeless. For migrant farm workers (the majority of whom are of Latin American descent), decent housing often is out of reach because their poor wages and undocumented status leave the workers vulnerable. In some circumstances, as many as twenty persons share unhealthy makeshift trailers as they move from locale to locale to earn a living harvesting crops that regularly fill supermarket shelves across the country.

Because of a requirement to limit terms of financial assistance, Bill Clinton's 1996 welfare reforms also exacerbated poor-quality housing. Among those becoming homeless are families who once received assistance but now are given term limits on their relief, often without sufficient support to help them transition into productive citizenship. In 1998, families leaving welfare rolls struggled to live and sometimes became homeless. Only a few found jobs paying livable wages. Most worked for low wages, often because they lacked training. Some lost jobs or had unstable employment because they needed child care.[6] One of the fastest-growing homeless groups is families with children, accounting for 33 percent of the homeless population. A significant number of these are women and children fleeing domestic violence.

After Hurricane Katrina, about 228,000 residences in New Orleans sustained flooding, in many cases including damage beyond repair. Thirty-nine percent of these residences were occupied by their owners, and 56 percent were rental residences. Seventy-five percent of persons in the flooded areas were African American, many of whom were poor and who doubt that they will be included in renewal of the city. Very recently sub-prime lending programs have affected families across income levels. In efforts to increase the numbers of loans underwritten, some mortgage companies offered borrowers below-prime adjustable mortgages that made it possible for persons to acquire homes far beyond their means. As the short terms of these loans ended, mortgage payments began to soar. The desire for excess on the part of lenders and borrowers means that with adjustments of the rates many families lost and are losing their homes. The history of housing in the United States and the recent issues persons face in accessing consistently secure, affordable, sufficient housing challenge the quality of social life across the society as well as the health of human resources for a vibrant democracy.

WHAT DOES IT MEAN TO BE FAITHFUL CHRISTIANS IN THE FACE OF AFFORDABLE HOUSING ISSUES?

What role do Christians have in responding to challenges persons face in acquiring consistently secure, affordable, sufficient housing? I want to highlight three ways of discussing Christian engagement with housing issues in our society. First, in accord with emphases in the Gospels on the "realm of God," Christians can take up practices that help bring forth signs of God's realm on earth. Second, reflecting the prominent moral norm asserted throughout Scripture, Christians have a responsibility to participate in practices of love. Finally, following the example of Jesus, whose ministry prominently featured occasions of healing and helping, Christians are called to bring healing to housing challenges faced by persons, families, and society.

What Is the "Realm of God"?

The phrase "realm of God" is most often translated in scripture as the "kingdom of God." However, the word translated in these texts as kingdom—*basileia*—refers first to the authority to reign rather than to a specific territory. The meaning conveyed is that God's presence can be known in evidence that God has authority.[7] In concord with this concept, the term "realm of God" conveys the idea of a sphere of divine influence, authority, and power. The Gospels are replete with references to the realm of God. They say it is a place to find lodging (Mark 4:30–32; Luke 13:18), belongs to the poor (Luke 6:20), and is a place of healing (Luke 9:2, 11; 10:9; Matt. 12:28; Luke 11:20). These references suggest that in the realm of God there is shelter, welcome for the poor, and remedy for sickness and the problems that persons face. In each case, the definition of the realm of God calls attention to places where conditions or circumstances can be improved for God's creatures. Being lodged, being included as a participant in something, and being healed all refer to changes that support and improve the quality of life. Some texts state plainly (e.g., Matt. 12:28; Luke 11:20) that when such changes occur, the realm of God is evident. Signs of the realm of God include changes that support and improve the quality of life.

Seeking to overcome challenges our society faces in providing all its citizens accessibility to consistently secure, affordable, sufficient housing coincides with bringing signs of the realm of God. Moreover, as the realm of God suggests a sphere broader than the individual person, problems of individuals as well as problems of society are relevant arenas of Christian activity in bringing forth signs of God's realm.

The Responsibility to Love

Perhaps the most important moral norm asserted throughout the Bible is the responsibility for persons to participate in practices of love. Many persons would even argue that the whole moral and ethical responsibility for Christians is summarized in the commandment to love. One explanation of the meaning of love in Christian tradition is presented in a passage from Scripture often referred to as the parable of the Good Samaritan. In this passage, as recorded in Luke 10, Jesus explains what it means to love one's neighbor by telling the story of the Samaritan who helps a wounded traveler. In the story, a man is robbed, beaten, and left near death. Two officials traveling the same way see the robbed man, but pass by him on the other side of the road. However, when the Samaritan sees the man, he comes near, is moved with compassion, and determines a course of action to address the man's situation. The Samaritan's determination includes attending to the man's immediate needs and devising an interim plan after the immediate needs are met. The interim plan apparently is necessary both because the robbed man requires further care and because the Samaritan has an agenda to which he must attend. In addition to recording Jesus telling this story to demonstrate what it means to love the neighbor, the writer's use of the term *agapao*ʿ is significant. The *agapao*ʿ of Luke 10:27 is not sentiment, feeling, or attraction as love often is defined. Instead, the term used in this passage means to love "in a social or moral sense," using the mind, the judgment, and the "will as a matter of principle" or as a matter of religious duty in order to manifest love.[8] Use of the mind, the judgment, and the will is what we see in the Samaritan's actions as he determines a response to the robbed man. Once he decides to act, the Samaritan uses his intellectual capacities as well as his financial resources. He bandages the man up, takes him to an inn, negotiates care for the man while he travels, and goes on to take up his own affairs with a plan to return to make sure the man is all right. These actions arise not simply from sentiment or charity. What we see in this story about love is an engagement of reason and will with emotion. Deliberation, intentionality, and conscious agency are all important resources in seeking to determine appropriate and lasting responses to the society's affordable housing challenges.

Offering Healing and Help

Finally, Christians are called to bring healing and help to our neighbors and to our society. All four Gospels include stories of Jesus healing persons and giving assistance to persons he encounters. It is, perhaps, self-evident that to follow Jesus means to offer healing and assistance where possible. Jesus cures paralysis

(Matt. 8:6–13), restores withered limbs (Matt. 12:10–13; Luke 6:10), heals lepers and the blind (Luke 17:14; Mark 10:52), stops hemorrhages (Luke 8:48), and remedies various other forms of illness.

In addition to healing these persons, Jesus assists other people with challenges they face. Jesus helps the woman taken in adultery (John 8:1–11) and Zacchaeus the tax collector (Luke 19:5–9) by accepting and engaging them. As he is preaching to the crowds, Jesus helps the fishermen who had toiled all night without success (Luke 5:1–10). In the story of the Good Samaritan, Jesus presents an example of giving assistance as a model of loving the neighbor.

An interesting element of many stories of Jesus healing and helping persons is the expectation Jesus had that they would immediately behave as agents taking action in their own lives. Jesus instructs the woman with the issue of blood to "go," the paralytic to "take up his bed," the man with the withered hand to "stretch forth," and the healed lepers to glorify God. In the case of Jesus helping the woman taken in adultery, Jesus challenges her accusers and her to live differently; in the story of Jesus assisting the potential disciples in their work of fishing, Jesus gives instructions about where to let down their nets for fish and later tells them they will fish for people. When Jesus assisted people, he was not only concerned that they receive help, but also that they take a role in changing their circumstances. Could it be that the healing and helping Jesus modeled took account of persons' emotional as well as physical circumstances? When we consider the role of Christians in engaging housing challenges, following Jesus' ministry of healing suggests that Christians are called to help heal the personal *and* social brokenness that prevent persons from taking actions in their circumstances as well as to provide immediate assistance in housing people.

HOW DO WE DELIBERATE ABOUT THESE ISSUES?

We can consider now three general ways Christians may engage housing issues by examining some specific issues at stake in regard to consistently secure, affordable, sufficient housing.

Affordable Housing and the Realm of God

Perhaps the most prominent characteristic of the realm of God is its identity as the arena of divine reign and influence. The persistence of homelessness and inadequate housing in our society does not reflect divine reign and influence. In view of the reality that there are persons who are homeless and who are occupying inadequate housing, one question raised for Christians is "Who counts?" On one level, the question "Who counts?" relates directly to the idea of the realm of God. One meaningful answer to the question is that everyone counts in the realm of God. Conceivably, one can say that the realm of God especially belongs to the poor. In 2005, there were over 38 million people living in poverty in the United States. The other level of the question "Who counts?" relates to the role of Christians as citizens of a democratic society in which persons experience housing challenges. Do homelessness and inadequate housing conflict with the principles of a progressive democracy? What does the persisting problem of homelessness say about who counts as citizens in our society?

The Responsibility to Love

A striking feature of the example of love presented by Jesus in the Good Samaritan story is the nature of the Samaritan's expression of love to the traveler. Engaging his judgment, his will, and his emotions, the Samaritan expressed love by determining a course of action that included use of his intellect, his finances, and his energy. Often the meaning of loving persons at the level of social engagement is conceived as related only to financial and physical resources. Giving money to worthy causes or giving time and energy through volunteerism to help build or repair a home, provide food, ensure transportation, and the like are traditional uses of financial and physical resources to address homelessness. However, caring for others through use of intellectual capacities may be the most significant way of expressing love, especially when such care can make the difference in another's quality of life. By using one's intellectual capacities it is possible to determine innovative courses of action that move beyond traditions of offering "charity" to persons in need of support. When love is thought of as including intellectual expression, new ideas and approaches to problems can arise that focus on immediate circumstances of individuals and, more importantly, address institutional and social factors that cause affordable housing problems. Do conceptions of what it means to love change when the starting point for loving someone includes engaging intellectual as well as volitional and emotional capacities? What might it mean to express love using intellectual capacities to respond to individual and social challenges with access to affordable housing?

Offering Healing and Help

The causes of homelessness and inadequate housing in the United States include social and personal factors: decreasing employment opportunities, family history of poverty, decreased public assistance, various forms of discrimination, limited access to social and financial resources, and catastrophes. The meaning of offering healing and help includes addressing all of these issues. Methods of offering help to individuals facing housing challenges may be imagined fairly effortlessly. If healing includes determining ways to empower persons to take charge of their lives, it may be more difficult to determine ways of offering healing to individuals and society. What does healing mean for persons and a society that continue to face housing challenges? What strategies and programs are necessary?

HOW TO GET INVOLVED

Many churches and individual Christians already participate in a range of activities that seek to address affordable housing issues. The remaining paragraphs highlight a variety of opportunities and resources for congregations and progressive Christians to engage in housing issues at local, state, and federal levels.

In 2000, the National Alliance to End Homelessness developed a plan to end homelessness in ten years. Entitled "A Plan, Not a Dream: How to End Homelessness in Ten Years," the program addresses ways to stop homelessness through prevention and housing. The plan proposes developing systemic responses to end homelessness, including boosting incomes, increasing affordable housing, and assisting persons who are homeless. Since the National Alliance announced its plan, ten-year efforts to end homelessness have been taken up by local, state, and national agencies across the country. Each includes its own decadelong design to end homelessness.

Many individuals and congregations annually undertake volunteer campaigns to build houses through the Habitat for Humanity housing programs. Begun in 1976, Habitat for Humanity seeks to address international housing issues by recruiting families and organizations to build family homes. Partnering organizations provide financial support and volunteers to complete work on the homes. Families selected qualify for a low-cost mortgage and help build their homes. Some criticisms of Habitat say the organization should provide upfront training and ongoing support to prepare persons for long-term home ownership. Without this support some families lose their homes or return to precarious economic circumstances.[9] A related criticism says that without focus on sustaining home ownership, the Habitat system becomes a mechanism of charity to soothe consciences of middle-class volunteers and donors. Should Habitat for Humanity partner to provide home owners with education and support at local levels while challenging the corporation to reintegrate such practices?

During the 1980s, significant increases in national homelessness rates led to lobbying and legislative proposals in Congress, finally resulting in the 1987 passage of the McKinney-Vento Homeless Assistance Act. The first major federal response to homelessness, McKinney-Vento originally called for emergency housing, transitional shelter, work training, healthcare, education, and permanent housing. A major contribution of McKinney-Vento was to remove the permanent address barrier to persons receiving Social Security, welfare, veterans assistance, food stamps, and Medicaid benefits. One important outgrowth of McKinney-Vento is the unfolding of the United States Interagency Council on Homelessness. Created by Congress to develop a federal approach to ending homelessness, the Interagency Council on Homelessness includes participation from eighteen federal agencies. Congregations can join Interagency efforts by engaging programs such as state and local ten-year plans to end homelessness and creating state Interagency councils.

Some persons and congregations support homeless and insufficiently housed persons through direct services such as providing meals and volunteers at local shelters. Still other congregations house persons in shelter sites they sponsor on and off their church campuses. One question recently raised about such work asks whether direct service agencies help sustain homeless lifestyles. In Atlanta, the mayor's office and the Metro Atlanta Task Force for the Homeless (the largest regional homeless shelters) are at odds regarding whether the Task Force's practices sustain homeless lifestyles and therefore run contrary to city and national efforts to end or at least significantly reduce chronic homelessness within the next decade.[10] How do we determine ways to ensure that our assistance for those who currently face housing needs does not contradict efforts to end the housing problems?

CONCLUSION

The challenge of overcoming affordable housing issues in the United States relates directly to the meaning of vibrancy of our democracy. What does "democracy" mean? Does democracy exist in a society that has an abundance of material and intellectual resources but will not overcome problems of persons living without consistent access to secure, affordable, sufficient housing? The health and vibrancy of a democracy—or any society—ultimately rests on the strength of its citizens. In view of this, self-interest suggests the need to change systems that weaken citizens and society. However, Christian churches and individual believers profess another reason for engaging housing issues. Their identity as people of God includes bringing signs of the divine realm, practicing love, and offering healing. As Christians bring to life these elements of their identity, they also help bring new life to the entire society.

QUESTIONS FOR DISCUSSION

1. What are some ways your congregation and denomination can address immediate housing needs of persons while supporting efforts to overcome the social issue of affordable housing and homelessness?
2. What forms of education are necessary to challenge the way persons think about economic issues related to housing such as living wages, parenting and child care, and healthcare access?

3. The inability to overcome some issues we confront often rests in our unwillingness to consider different ways of structuring our life together. What are some innovative programs for addressing society's housing issues? How can your congregation become involved in these?
4. Do you have consistent access to secure, affordable, sufficient housing? If so, identify and make a list of ways your life would change if you did not have this access. Discuss with members of your congregation ways to address items on your list.

RESOURCES

Books

Berck, Judith. *No Place to Be: Voices of Homeless Children*. Boston: Houghton Mifflin, 1992.

De Souza Briggs, Xavier N., and William Julius Wilson. *The Geography of Opportunity: Race and Housing Choice in Metropolitan America*. Washington, DC: Brookings Institute, 2005.

Loewen, James W. *Sundown Towns: A Hidden Dimension of American Racism*. New York: New Press, 2005.

Reckford, Jonathan T. M. *Creating a Habitat for Humanity: No Hands But Yours*. Minneapolis: Fortress, 2007.

Turner, Margery Austin, and Sheila R. Zedlewski, eds. *After Katrina: Rebuilding Opportunity and Equity into the New New Orleans*. Washington, DC: Urban Institute, 2006.

Web Sites

National Alliance to End Homelessness, www.endhomelessness.org/.

National Low Income Housing Coalition, http://www.nlihc.org.

United States Office of Housing and Urban Development, http://www.hud.gov/offices/cpd/affordablehousing.

The Urban Institute, www.urban.org/housing/index.cfm.

NOTES

1. Jonathan T. M. Reckford, *Creating a Habitat for Humanity: No Hands But Yours* (Minneapolis: Fortress, 2007), 59, 47.
2. Http://www.hud.gov/offices/cpd/affordablehousing.
3. James W. Loewen, *Sundown Towns: A Hidden Dimension of American Racism* (New York: Touchstone, 2005), 9–10.
4. Saul Feldman, "Out of the Hospital, onto the Streets: The Overselling of Benevolence," *The Hastings Center Report* 13, no. 3 (June 1983): 5; National Coalition for the Homeless, "Who is Homeless" NCH Fact Sheet #3, www.nationalhomeless.org.

5. Peter Dreier, "Reagan's Legacy: Homelessness in America," *Shelterforce Online*, Issue 135, May/June 2004, http://www.nhi.org/online/issues/135/reagan.html.
6. Children's Defense Fund and National Coalition for the Homeless, *Welfare to What: Early Findings on Family Hardship and Wellbeing* (Washington, DC: National Coalition for the Homeless, 1998).
7. Since the word in these texts translated as kingdom—"basileia"—refers to the authority to reign rather than to a specific territory, I use the phrase "realm of God" to convey the idea of a sphere of divine authority and power. See James Strong, *The Exhaustive Concordance of the Bible* (Nashville: Abingdon, 1980), 18.
8. Strong, *Exhaustive Concordance,* 7, 76.
9. Mara Der Hovanesian, Greg Hafkin, and Christopher Palmeri, "Habitat for Hustlers: Freewheeling Lenders Seen Preying on Families in Affordable-Home Program," *Business Week Online*, November 10, 2006.
10. Lyle V. Harris, "Homelessness: It'll Take a Team," *The Atlanta Journal-Constitution, Sunday*, August 5, 2007.

Chapter 10

For All Creation

GRACE Y. KAO

Taking action on behalf of the environment has become trendy. Former Vice President Al Gore won an Academy Award for his 2006 documentary about global climate change. Hollywood celebrities now aspire to buy hybrid-electric vehicles like Toyota Priuses. Articles and quizzes regularly appear in mainstream news outlets and other popular media about reducing our "ecological footprint," or the amount of natural resources our patterns of consumption require. Still others implore us to become "carbon neutral" by balancing our carbon dioxide emissions through producing equal amounts of useful energy (e.g., planting trees) or by buying "carbon offsets" for others to do the same. Even organic foods and products—the vast majority of which some twenty years ago were only available at small health-food and specialty stores—have corporatized, gone mainstream, and can be found on the shelves of regular supermarkets and retail giants such as Wal-Mart. Everybody, it now seems, feels the push to become more "green."

It should come as no surprise that Christians have taken part in this cultural shift toward eco-consciousness as well. The proposed Social Creed for the Twenty-first Century affirms the prophetic witness of the historic Social Creed of the Churches of 1908, which was adopted at the founding of the Federal Council of Churches (the predecessor of the National Council of Churches in Christ [NCC]) and was dedicated, among other things, to the "preservation, enhancement, and faithful" use of the "natural world as God's handiwork." Other recent ecumenical statements, including the World Council of Church's (WCC) 2005 Alternative Globalization Addressing Peoples and Earth (AGAPE) and the World Alliance of Reformed Church's (WARC) 2004 Covenanting for Justice in the Economy and the Earth, have reaffirmed the biblical ideas of God's sovereignty over all of creation (Ps. 24:1) and that of the earth "groaning" for its liberation because of the ways we humans continue to exploit it (Rom. 8:19–22). Even portions of American evangelical Christianity—a segment that has traditionally looked askance at environmentalism and even associated it with contemporary pagan nature worship—have recently defended the environment as a moral issue, promoted "creation care" to combat global warming, and campaigned against gas-guzzling SUVs with strategically placed advertisements that ask "What Would Jesus Drive?"

Indeed, as awareness of and conscientiousness about the disastrous effects of global climate change increase among the general public, much environmental advocacy has been directed toward the transportation sector. Especially when coupled with consumer concerns about the rising cost of gasoline, more and more Americans are walking, biking, taking public transportation, or carpooling to work and other important functions instead of driving a single-occupancy vehicle. While changing individual habits is essential to reducing energy use, governments and institutions must also step up to provide the infrastructure necessary to facilitate this shift. My own institution, Virginia Tech, has a highly efficient and widely used public transit system, a pilot program in vanpooling, a youth-oriented ridesharing program that aims to turn social networks into travel networks, and a Commuter Alternatives Program (CAP) that provides financial incentives, preferred parking spaces, and emergency ride home services for students and faculty who either carpool to school or regularly bike, bus, or walk. These programs reportedly save us Hokies $839,777 a year on gas, reduce CO_2 emissions by about 2,531 metric tons a year, and have earned us a spot on the Environmental Protection Agency's first annual list of "Best Workplaces for Commuters" among colleges and universities.[1] Since CO_2 emissions represent approximately 75 percent of the greenhouse gases that contribute to global warming, and since the United States is responsible for roughly 25 percent of that global CO_2 total—with emissions from gas vehicles alone constituting about 20 percent of that U.S. total—it is imperative that we radically reduce the environmental damage caused by our dominant "car culture." Indeed, we Americans make up only 4.6 percent of the world's population, but own and drive approximately 24 percent of the world's cars![2]

GLOBAL LIVESTOCK PRODUCTION AS AN ENVIRONMENTAL AND SOCIAL CONCERN

Given the widespread attention directed toward issues related to transportation, it may come as a surprise that the Food and Agriculture Organization of the United Nations (UNFAO) recently concluded that the global livestock sector generates 18 percent of total greenhouse gas emissions as measured in CO_2 equivalent, which is an even higher share than global transport. More specifically, the production of global livestock is responsible for 37 percent of methane and 65 percent of nitrous oxide emissions—and these gases have 23 and 296 times the Global Warming Potential (GWP) of carbon dioxide, respectively. Such emissions stem from various natural and industrialized processes throughout the entire meat commodity chain. Feed production involves the burning of fossil fuels to produce chemical fertilizers, land-use changes for grazing and feedcrops, and land degradation through overgrazing, compacting, and erosion caused by livestock action. In animal production, carbon dioxide is released by the livestock through ordinary respiration, methane by the belches and flatulence of ruminants (like cows and sheep) through a digestive process called enteric fermentation, and both methane and nitrous oxide from manure and waste management. Of course, the processing and transportation of animals and animal products from either pasture or industrialized feedlots to slaughterhouses and meatpacking plants and then to consumer markets requires additional fossil fuel use.[3]

Beyond its contribution to global warming, this sector significantly degrades water and land and leads to a loss of biodiversity. Global livestock production uses approximately 8 percent of the earth's increasingly scarce water resources, mostly to irrigate feedcrops, and pollutes rivers, lakes, streams, and groundwater by spills or breaks in manure lagoons in cases of extreme weather or simply when animal wastes cannot be successfully contained because too many animals are being confined to too small a space. Antibiotics and hormones used on livestock, chemicals from fertilizers and pesticides, and sediments from eroded pastures are also leaching into local water sources. Such water pollution not only leads to serious human illnesses, disease, and antibiotic resistance, but also manure-related fish kills, "dead" zones in coastal areas, and the degradation of coral reefs. Finally, with respect to dwindling biodiversity, the UNFAO estimates that species loss is running fifty to five hundred times higher than background rates found in the fossil record and that the one-third of the Earth's land surface now dedicated to livestock production, which includes 70 percent of the former forests in the Amazon that have been razed for this purpose, was once habitat for wildlife. It appears, then, that decreasing the adverse environmental impact of global meat consumption is at least as important as addressing transportation issues, if not more so.

But how did we get in this predicament? Traditionally, farms practiced more sustainable forms of agriculture: farmers promoted biodiversity by growing a variety of crops (not monocultures) for direct human consumption; used animal manure for organic fertilizer and the animals themselves both for work (i.e., pulling loads) and as food; and fed the animals locally available feed, such as grass, hay, and crop wastes that had no value to humans as food. When both agriculture and meat production underwent a process of intensification, industrialization, and corporate consolidation in the United States in the second half of the twentieth century, agribusinesses increasingly fed their livestock market-traded feed concentrates such as corn, geographically separated feed production from animal production, and crammed massive quantities of animals into Concentrated Animal Feeding Operations (CAFOs) or "factory farms." In addition, refrigeration permitted processed meat, not just live animals, to be shipped from factory farms to meatpacking plants and then to markets and thereby increased production. Urbanization, population growth, and comparable processes of industrialization that have occurred in other parts of the world have further augmented the global demand for meat and meat products. The worldwide consumption of meat has doubled since 1980 and is expected to double again in the next fifty years, as is the expected output of milk. This exponential but ecologically unsustainable growth has led the same UNFAO report to conclude that the "environmental costs per unit of livestock production must be cut by one half, just to avoid the level of damage worsening beyond its present level."

Unfortunately, global livestock production not only raises the aforementioned environmental calamities, but also a host of other serious human health and social problems. Consider the billion-dollar pork industry in the United States. Pigs now outnumber people in North Carolina, the number two hog-producing state in the country. Industrial hog operations now control at least 75 percent of the market and have accordingly forced many small hog farmers out of business. According to the USDA's National Agricultural Statistics Service, there has been a twenty-four-year decline in the number of hog farm operations with an increase in the average size of those still operating, such that in 2006 only 5 percent of the inventory came from operations with 1–499 head and 54 percent from those with 5,000 or more (and 115 operations with 50,000+). These mega-farms produce air pollutants and objectionable odors from ammonia nitrogen and hydrogen sulfide from animal wastes that adversely affect the health and well-being of those living nearby. Studies have shown that those living in proximity to these "swine cities" report more tension, depression, anger, fatigue, and confusion, and less overall vigor than control subjects; suffer higher levels of upper-respiratory and gastrointestinal problems than even those living near large cattle farms; and contract even more chronic health problems such as bronchitis if working on the hog farms themselves. What is more, the presence of CAFOs significantly reduces land and property values within a one- to three-mile radius. Still worse is the fact that a higher percentage of these industrial hog operations have been located in politically weak and low-income communities with sizable African American and Native American populations, thus raising serious questions of environmental injustice and institutional racism.

Finally, these social and environmental justice issues can be further compounded when we consider the shifting demographics and working conditions of the meatpacking worker today. Unlike in the 1960s and 1970s, when the average meatpacker was white, middle-class, and unionized and received roughly 14–20 percent more in salary than in manufacturing jobs, union membership has plummeted since the 1980s and salaries are now approximately 20–30 percent less than those offered in manufacturing jobs. Many meatpackers today also lack a high school degree and increasingly come undocumented from Mexico, Central America, and Southeast Asia to work in what the U.S. Bureau of Labor Statistics has consistently reported as either the or one of the most dangerous jobs in the country. Worse still, according to Human Rights Watch (HRW), is that meat industry employers in the United States routinely put their workers at predictable risk of serious physical injury, frustrate their efforts to receive compensation for workplace injuries, aggressively block their self-organizing efforts and freedom of association, and thereby systematically violate their human rights.[4]

WHAT IS TO BE DONE?

Alleviating the serious problems caused by global livestock production will require specific public policy initiatives and reforms, such as greater protection of wildlife habitats, the use of tax credits and conservation easements to address the loss of biodiversity, increased regulation and stricter standards for waste disposal and clean-up (e.g., the banning of new open-air manure lagoons and aerial spraying of liquid wastes), and an enhanced commitment to the findings of Environmental Impact Studies. It may also require advancements in technology, such as improved efficiency of irrigation systems to address water depletion. Changes of the magnitude required for the sake of a healthy environment will certainly necessitate profound attitudinal and economic shifts as well, since we simply cannot continue these destructive patterns of production and consumption.

In short, we need a major overhaul in the way ordinary business is conducted in this sector. In particular, we must put an end to the socially irresponsible and environmentally destructive subsidies that encourage farmers to overuse and overproduce. More specifically, beginning in the 1970s, U.S. food policy fiscally encouraged farmers to produce certain commodity crops such as corn and soybeans. Instead of managing the supply or limiting production and thus stabilizing prices, successive USDA farm bills further encouraged these farmers to put all of their commodity crops on the market each year—and then heavily subsidized them so that they could be sold domestically and internationally for demonstrably less than it actually costs to grow them. And yet, it has not been the farmers themselves who have primarily benefited from these policies, but the large-scale agribusinesses that then purchase these artificially cheap crops to feed their factory-farmed animals, or else flood them on the international market under the banner of free trade, thereby contributing to the impoverishment of rural corn farmers in Mexico, among others. When we as taxpayers subsidize these commodity crops, we are inadvertently supporting the very cycle of social and environmental ills that do us in America and elsewhere so much harm.

To be sure, we as consumers may think we are benefiting from the industrialization of meat that the farm bill encourages. After all, we Americans have significantly increased our meat consumption in the past several decades (we consumed roughly two hundred pounds of meat per person in 2005, which is twenty-two pounds more than in 1970 and sixty-eight pounds more than in 1945) while paying progressively less for it (the price of beef today is about half, in real dollar terms, of what it was in the 1970s).[5] But once we are better informed about meat's true cost, our continued participation in this system makes us complicitous in the ways we externalize or collectively pass off the real, hidden environmental and social costs of production onto others: the meatpackers who are exploited when they do this dangerous work; the family farmers and surrounding communities (both domestically and in the two-thirds world) whose livelihoods and well-being are adversely affected by the operations of these mega-corporations and by these export subsidies; and the environment itself, in the form of the water and soil degradation, greenhouse gas emissions, damage to ecosystems, and loss of biodiversity discussed previously.

THEOLOGY'S CONTRIBUTION AND THE INTRINSIC VALUE OF ALL OF CREATION

From the perspective of Christian ethics, the Bible offers a visionary and trenchant approach to thinking about our environmental problems in the form of covenantal theology and jubilee justice. Not only does human-initiated ecological devastation cause the most vulnerable among us to suffer disproportionately and cause demonstrable harm to future generations, but our environmental sins also violate the entire creation with which God continues to be in covenantal relationship. More specifically, we learn in Genesis 9:9–10 that God established an enduring covenant with the living creatures that were with Noah—the fowl, cattle, and other beasts of the earth—and not simply with Noah and his descendants. We also learn from Leviticus 25:23 and Psalm 24:1

that the earth and all that is in it is the Lord's and thus can neither be commodified, nor treated as simply "our" natural resource. The Sabbath traditions further reveal that the rest required one day each week was not only intended for humans, but also for the animals and the land, just as the sabbatical year requiring the land, vineyards, and olive groves to lie fallow was for the poor to be able to eat as well as for the wild animals to do the same afterward (Exod. 23:10–12). The jubilee tradition likewise mandated rest for the land itself, in addition to prohibiting any permanent institution of Hebrew slavery and requiring both the cancellation of debts and the restoring of those who had been previously alienated. Finally, we would be wise to remember that Jesus connected his own ministry with this jubilee tradition when he read from the Isaiah scroll in Galilee (Lev. 25:8–55; Isa. 61:2; Luke 4:14–30). Thus, whatever philosophical or theological debates may remain about the moral status of individual animals, entire species, or whole ecosystems, it seems clear that the people of God have been enjoined to recognize the intrinsic value of creation and not simply its instrumental use.

There are, of course, many ways that we can translate this theological vision of the intrinsic worth and importance of all of God's creation into public policy beyond the specific call I have issued in this chapter concerning global livestock production and American food policy. For example, some evangelical and mainline Protestant Christians who partnered with Jewish and other religious community organizations to form the Noah Alliance have focused their energies instead on preserving a strong Endangered Species Act (ESA), in light of recent Congressional proposals to weaken and amend it. Still others, like the growing movement of environmentally active Catholic nuns in Canada and North America, known as the "green sisters" or the Sisters of the Earth movement, have adopted additional concrete ways to heal the earth. They are modeling sustainability by using renewable materials to build alternative lodgings, building solidarity by engaging in community-supported organic gardens, turning their communal properties into land trusts with wildlife sanctuaries, and otherwise taking a prophetic stand for the sanctity of creation by disrupting shareholder meetings of corporate polluters, leading struggles to stop the proliferation of suburban sprawl, opposing the spread of genetically modified organisms (GMOs), and conserving heirloom seeds. While environmental activism of these kinds may mean that some human and commercial interests may have to take a backseat, responsible care and stewardship of the earth as God's handiwork arguably requires such action.

As essays throughout this book detail, significant social change requires personal and public accountability. We must transform our personal lifestyle habits as well as work together to create structural change. I conclude with three concrete suggestions for how congregations can get involved in environmental social change at the local level.

WAYS TO GET INVOLVED AND TAKE ACTION

First, for people in positions to influence church leadership, consider ways to integrate ecology into the liturgy beyond a once-in-a-while prayer for the environment or an annual St. Francis of Assisi or Earth Day celebration. Ecofeminist theologian Rosemary Radford Ruether has suggested that we adopt a "creational consciousness,"[6] so that we do not view the rest of the created world as merely inert objects or "resources" for our own use, but as standing in a direct and intimate relationship with God (Pss. 104; 65:5–13; Job 38–40:2). Such consciousness raising might require repentance for our arrogance or even the cultivation of a sense of horror at the devastating ecological consequences of our failures of responsible care and stewardship (Isa. 24). An ecologically conscious liturgical calendar might also involve special emphases in different seasons: Easter as a celebration of the resurrection of Christ and of nature in springtime, Thanksgiving as a period of gratitude to God for nature's bounty and other blessings, and perhaps even an incorporation of Arbor Day as a time to commit to tree planting in deforested areas.

Second, consider focusing your advocacy on local environmental issues, not out of any myopic NIMBY ("not in my backyard") principle, but because grassroots activism cultivates a sense of communal responsibility and solidarity and can be particularly effective in bringing about social change. For instance, in the Appalachian region where I currently live, a grassroots organization called Christians for the Mountains is working against the grave ecological and social devastation caused by the mountaintop removal of our "purple mountain majesties" by large coal-mining corporations. Among other initiatives, they are urging elected representatives to support the Clean Water Protection Act, H.R. 2169 (2007–2008, 110th Congress), so as to prevent the mining industry from dumping industrial wastes into streams and rivers under the guise of renaming it as "fill."

If you are unaware of the most pressing environmental concerns of your particular region or community, consider doing your part in maintaining access to clean, sufficient, and affordable water for the sake of human rights and environmental justice, so as to keep water in public trust—not corporate control. You can do this by advocating for stricter local and state groundwater laws to protect aquifers and other water resources, monitoring city agencies or mayor's offices for signs of impending water privatization initiatives, requiring local and/or state referendums regarding the privatization of water or sewage, and of course, altering your own drinking habits so that you avoid the unnecessary consumption of bottled water. In the summer of 2007, given concerns about fiscal responsibility, habitat protection, and global warming, the Stockton, California, City Council unanimously reversed its February 2003 water privatization agreement, and the mayor of San Francisco banned the city government, city concessions, and all city-funded events and functions from using city money to buy bottled water. Might these examples of regional activism encourage you to lobby for something similar in your own community?

Third, do what you can to educate yourself about the ways in which the USDA Farm Bill, which is renewed about every five years in Congress, dramatically affects not only domestic food policy and the industrialization of meat, but also the availability and cost of food abroad and thus global poverty. As Michael Pollan, author of *The Omnivore's Dilemma*, has noted, it will take imaginative policy making to reform the USDA Farm Bill in such a way as to encourage our farmers to focus on sustainable agriculture instead of on all-out production, to grow real food for direct human consumption and not simply feed for livestock or industrial raw materials for food manufacturers and processors, and to rebuild local food economies. An example of the type of necessary structural reform can be found in the National Family Farms Coalition (NFFC)–developed Food from Family Farms Act (FFFA) of 2007, which was designed to reverse the effacement of sustainable and diversified family farms by huge corporate crop plantations and factory farms that depend upon vast amounts of fossil fuel energy use, exploited labor, harmful technologies, and substantial taxpayer subsidies for their success.

While working for structural change through farm bill reform and in light of the fact that the industrialized food we eat in America, on average, travels thirteen hundred to two thousand miles before it reaches our plates, consider supporting your local or regional community food system (wherein the growing, harvesting, processing, packaging, transporting, advertising, consuming, and disposing of food and any associated packaging are designed to enhance the social, economic, and environmental health of a particular place). The goal would be to internalize as many of those externalities as you could. You might participate in a community, church, or school garden or kitchen; buy a share in a Community-Supported Agriculture (CSA) farm; commit to a diet heavily sourced in local, organic, and sustainably grown, raised, and/or processed foods (which will entail patronizing stores, farmers' markets, co-ops, and restaurants that offer them); reduce or eliminate entirely your consumption of meat, eggs, and dairy products that originate from factory farms and corporate agribusinesses; and encourage your church to model these very changes (e.g., might the wine or juice and bread used for the Eucharist/Holy Communion/Lord's Supper originate locally?).

Admittedly, until and unless there is significant structural reform in our food and agricultural policy, the aforementioned suggestions will require not insignificant sacrifices on our pocketbooks, let alone other inconvenient lifestyle changes. But such is the call of the proposed Social Creed for the Twenty-first Century, as the pledge to be stewards will require us to work jointly for the adoption of simpler lifestyles for those who have enough; wise care of land and technology so that all might have access to clean air, water, and healthy food; sustainable use of Earth's resources and promotion of alternative energy sources and sustainable public transportation; and equitable global trade and aid that protects local economies, initiatives, cultures, and livelihoods.

QUESTIONS FOR DISCUSSION

1. What practical difference would it make to you, your family, or your church community if you began to view all of creation—not just humans—as intrinsically valuable and as standing in a covenantal relationship with God? What aspects of your lifestyle or patterns of consumption would you feel the most convicted about transforming? Would you be prompted to support or reject certain public policies, initiatives, or campaigns? Which ones?
2. Consider all of the things that you, your family, or your church community normally does, consumes, or otherwise uses up in a typical week (food, other material goods, gas, electricity for lighting, cooling, and heating). In what ways does your current lifestyle impose upon others and upon the environment? How can you reduce or internalize these externalities? If you do not know the answers to these questions, how might you go about finding out?
3. What is causing or making a serious and negative environmental impact on your local community and surrounding neighborhoods? How might you do your personal and communal part to remedy the situation? If you do not know the answers to these questions, what specifically can and will you do to find out?

RESOURCES

Books

Berry, Thomas. *The Dream of the Earth*. San Francisco: Sierra Club Books with the University of California Press, 1988.

Rasmussen, Larry. *Earth Community, Earth Ethics*. Maryknoll, NY: Orbis, 1996.

Ruether, Rosemary Radford. *Gaia and God: Ecofeminism and Earth Healing*. San Francisco: HarperSanFrancisco, 1992.

Web Sites

Earth Ministry, http://www.earthministry.org.

The National Council of Churches of Christ (NCC) Eco-Justice Programs, http://www.nccecojustice.org/index.htm.

The National Religious Partnership on the Environment (NRPE), http://www.nrpe.org/.

United Nations Food and Agricultural Organization, www.fao.org.

NOTES

1. Greg Esposito, "Virginia Tech Gets Nod for Aiding Commuters," *Roanoke Times*, May 23, 2006.
2. These percentages are based upon the following sources: (1) Global Warming Potential (GWP) of CO_2: United Nations Environment Programme's (UNEP) Intergovernmental Panel on Climate Change (IPCC); (2) U.S. and global CO_2 emissions from transportation: *U.S. Department of Energy Data Book*, 26th ed. (2007); (3) U.S. and world car ownership: 2007 National Transportation Statistics of the U.S. Department of Transportation Bureau of Transportation Statistics (BTS) and the World Bank; (4) U.S. and world population: CIA *World Factbook* (July 2007 estimate).
3. Henning Steinfield et al., "Livestock's Long Shadow: Environmental Issues and Options" (Rome: United Nations Food and Agricultural Organization, 2006), available at http://www.fao.org/newsroom/en/news/2006/1000448/index.html.
4. Lance Compa et al., "Blood, Sweat, and Fear: Workers' Rights in U.S. Meat and Poultry Plants" (New York: Human Rights Watch, 2005), available at http://www.hrw.org/reports/2005/usa0105/.
5. These figures are taken from February 15, 2007 statistics of the USDA Economic Research Service (ERS).
6. Rosemary Radford Ruether, "Ecological Theology: Roots in Tradition, Liturgical, and Ethical Practice for Today," *Dialog: A Journal of Theology* 42, no. 3 (2003): 226–34.

Chapter 11

For Alternatives to War and Militarism

GARY DORRIEN

One of the central problems of U.S. American Christian ethics today is how to confront the growing U.S. militarism and imperialism.[1] Historically, U.S. Americans have resisted the idea that their country has any such problem. The term "militarism" bears a mostly pejorative connotation in Christian ethics and U.S. society, suggesting an excessive exaltation of war, martial values, and the military establishment, while the term "empire" is even more foreign to the United States' idea of itself as a benevolent republic.

In the classic sense of the term, setting aside the Native American reservations, the United States is not an empire. It does not exercise direct dominion over conquered peoples. It does not formally rule an extensive group of countries under a single sovereign authority. In most cases the United States favors democracy and self-determination for other nations. The official U.S. colonies have been few and scattered, most of its occupations have been brief, the largest of its fourteen dependent entities is Puerto Rico, and its domination of Latin America has been mostly indirect. Most U.S. Americans have little imperial consciousness, and they are not militaristic in the sense of glorying in their wars or military might.

Yet the United States has been on a neo-imperial trajectory since its founding. It conquered nearly an entire continent and waged genocidal violence against Native Americans, colonizing the surviving tribes in reservations. For almost ninety years the United States was a slave state, many of whose leaders wanted to create a Western empire based on the extension of slavery throughout the Caribbean. From the Monroe Doctrine to the Bush Doctrine, presidents have pronounced their putative right to dominate or invade sovereign nations. Theodore Roosevelt, who viewed his imperial ambition as a natural outgrowth of the U.S. American story, was fond of saying that his country's entire national history was one of expansion. His corollary to the Monroe Doctrine, announced in 1906, declared that the United States was entitled to invade any Latin American nation that engaged in "flagrant wrongdoing." Latin Americans took that to mean any action that conflicted with U.S. interests.

Long before the Roosevelt Corollary was announced, the United States had an ample record of intervening in Latin America. In 1898, it escalated to old-fashioned imperialism—the colonization of overseas territories—by annexing and occupying Cuba, Puerto Rico, Guam, the Philippines, and the Hawaiian islands. Afterward, up to World War II, the United States added interventions in Colombia, Panama, Honduras, the Dominican Republic, Cuba, Nicaragua, Haiti, Mexico, and Guatemala, in addition to "making the world safe for democracy" by intervening in World War I; China was another frequent destination of American forces.

In 1945, the United States began to amass a global military empire, beginning with its new military bases in western Germany, Japan, Korea, and the eastern Mediterranean. In 1989, having emerged from the Cold War as the world's only superpower, the United States began to debate what it should do with its unrivaled might. Powerful currents in U.S. American politics and the defense industry called for a foreign policy of global supremacy; neoconservatives put it explicitly, espousing a doctrine of global military hegemony called "unipolarism" or "full spectrum dominance." This country has forged a new kind of empire that dwarfs all colonizing empires of the past, one not based on the conquest of territory. The United States routinely engages in imperial practices under Republican and Democratic administrations alike, and in the neoconservative wing of the Republican Party the rhetoric of imperial domination could not be more explicit.

The United States is the most awesome world power that the world has ever seen. Its economy outproduces the next eleven nations combined, accounting for 32 percent of the world's output. It floods the world with its culture and technology. It spends more on defense, officially, than the next 25 nations combined. When total military spending is taken into account, it outspends the rest of the world combined. It employs five global military commands to police the world; it has 750 military bases in 130 countries, covering two-thirds of the world; it has formal military base rights in forty countries; each branch of the armed services has its own air force; the U.S. Air Force operates on six continents; the United States deploys carrier battleships in every ocean; and the U.S. Special Forces conducts thousands of operations per year in approximately 170 nations.

Moreover, the United States is not merely dominant; it assumes imperial responsibilities and reaps the benefits that derive from them. It is imperial in the sense of enforcing its idea of world order in its own interest, presuming the right to lay down the rules of trade, commerce, security, and political legitimacy. It rewards or punishes nations on the basis of their willingness to create open markets, support U.S. military policies, and establish pro-U.S. governments.

After invading Iraq in 2003, the United States radically redesigned Iraq's economy, ignoring longstanding Iraqi laws that limited foreign ownership and principles of international law that limit the powers of occupiers. In May 2003, Paul Bremer banned thirty thousand former Baath Party leaders from employment in Iraq's public sector and disbanded the Iraqi Army, decisions that became controversial for disastrously fueling the Sunni insurgency against the United States. But in the same month Bremer took other drastic measures that were rarely noted. He abolished nearly all of Iraq's laws, issuing a hundred binding decrees that sold off state enterprises, suspended tariffs on imports and exports, allowed for 100 percent foreign ownership of Iraqi businesses, reduced corporate taxes to 15 percent, and permitted businesses to repatriate 100 percent of their profits. Somehow all of this was taken for granted as the spoils of empire, even as the United States denied being one. Waging an offensive war to change the government of a sovereign nation and restructure its economy is an imperial enterprise. Doing it to consolidate one's power and change the political culture of a sprawling, explosive, multinational region halfway around the globe is more so on a staggering scale, with staggering costs.

One of the central problems of U.S. foreign policy today is how to modulate the natural tendency of an unrivaled power to regard the entire world as its geopolitical neighborhood. This would have been a defining challenge for the administration of George W. Bush even if terrorists had not struck the United States on September 11, 2001. At the turn of the twenty-first century, the United States was overdue for a moral and political reckoning with the compulsive expansionism of unrivaled power. But the problem of militarized empire increased by several orders of magnitude with Bush's election in 2000, his selection of a neoconservative foreign policy team, their urging after the fiendish attacks of 9/11 to conceive the struggle against terrorism as a world war, and his decision to do so.

In the early 1990s, neoconservatives called for a foreign policy of global dominion. Instead of cutting back on military spending and foreign military bases, they argued, the United States needed to expand its military reach to every region of the world, creating an American-dominated world order. *Washington Post* columnist Charles Krauthammer called it "unipolarism." Ben Wattenberg, a senior fellow at the American Enterprise Institute in Washington,

D.C., called it "unipolarism," and added "neo–Manifest Destinarianism." William Kristol, editor of the *Weekly Standard*, and Robert Kagan, cofounder of the Project for the New American Century, called it "benevolent global hegemony." Other leading neocons included Paul Wolfowitz, Richard Perle, Norman Podhoretz, Midge Decter, Irving Kristol, Michael Novak, Jeane Kirkpatrick, Joshua Muravchik, Frank Gaffney, Zalmay Khalilzad, Doug Feith, Michael Ledeen, and George Weigel. From the beginning there were key differences between the movement's nationalistic-realist wing (led by Krauthammer, Kirkpatrick, and Irving Kristol) and its democratic-globalist wing (led by Wolfowitz, Wattenberg, and William Kristol) over the importance of exporting democracy, but all neocons who made the transition to post–Cold War unipolarism agreed that the fundamental objective of U.S. foreign policy was to prevent any nation or group of nations from becoming a great power rival.[2]

By the late 1990s, the neoconservatives were the strongest foreign policy faction in the Republican Party, having forged alliances with old-style conservative hawks such as Dick Cheney and Donald Rumsfeld. In September 2000, a group of leading neocons hoping for positions in a Republican administration issued a position paper that spelled out the particulars of a global empire strategy: repudiate the ABM treaty; build a global missile defense system; develop a strategic dominance of space; increase defense spending by $20 billion per year; establish permanent new forces in southern Europe, Southeast Asia, and the Middle East; and reinvent the U.S. military to "fight and decisively win multiple, simultaneous major theater wars."[3] They also remarked that it might take "a new Pearl Harbor" for Americans to realize the necessity of a global dominion strategy.

When George W. Bush won the presidency, the neocons came with him, mostly on Cheney's influence. Bush himself knew little about international issues, and his early foreign policy was a patchwork of neoconservative and conservative-realist positions. He expected to spend his presidency oscillating between the views of Wolfowitz and Condoleezza Rice, his mentors during the campaign. But on September 11, 2001, the president needed a worldview. He was surrounded by people who had one; they were obsessed with invading Iraq, and by then, so was he. Bush and his senior officials had a privileged vision of what was going to happen in Iraq that they did not allow to be challenged: American power would quickly prevail and a pro-U.S. regime led by Iraqi exile leader Ahmed Chalabi or someone like him would be readily installed. Four years later the United States had 160,000 troops bogged down in a miserable, murderous war in Iraq, where a nightmarish insurgency has morphed into something worse, a many-sided civil war raging under the constraints of foreign occupation.

As this chapter is being written, the United States is spending $2 billion per week in Iraq, nearly all of it from emergency spending bills, which exceeded $500 billion by August 2007. These figures do not include disability and health payments for returning troops, inducements for soldiers to serve additional deployments, extra pay for reservists and National Guard members, and additional foreign aid to supportive nations. When all of that is factored in, along with the Pentagon's unprecedented dependence on expensive private contractors, the bill for five years of Iraq is expected to be $2 trillion, all of it added to the federal debt, which comes out to eighteen thousand dollars per household.

The defense budget for 2008, which covers normal personnel, procurement, and operational expenses, is up to $461 billion. In addition to not including the costs of the wars in Iraq and Afghanistan, this figure does not include nuclear weapons ($22 billion, assigned to the Energy Department) or the defense expenditures of the National Defense Stockpile, Selective Service, FBI, and Coast Guard (approximately $5 billion). Neither does it count the State Department's security programs ($38 billion), homeland security programs not in the Pentagon budget ($36 billion), the human costs of past and current wars handled by the Department of Veterans Affairs ($84 billion), or interest payments on the national debt related to defense spending ($75 billion), plus miscellaneous expenditures in other agencies. When these items are counted, total military spending for 2008 comes to approximately $885 billion.

Despite these immense outlays, budget analysts warn of a coming financial train wreck, because the appropriations in virtually every category fall short of the true costs of the nation's military posture. The United States is caught in the classic imperial dilemma of spending fantastic sums on the military yet lacking enough military to cover its foreign policy. In November 2006, Army chief of staff General Peter Schoomaker withheld his required 2008 budget plan as a protest against what his staff called a "disastrous" and "unsustainable" situation in the army. The army's regular budget in 2007 was $99 billion, but Schoomaker demanded a 41 percent increase, eventually settling for 19 percent, which included a 55 percent increase in procurement. Having been limited by law to 482,400 troops in the 1990s, the army added 30,000 troops on a temporary basis in 2004, which became permanent. At the time of this writing, an army expansion of 65,000 troops is making its way through Congress, fueled politically by the army's struggle to sustain rotations in Iraq and its institution of what amounted to a backdoor draft by relying on the National Guard and extending many tours of duty. At present over half of the Army's forty-three combat brigades are deployed overseas.

Donald Rumsfeld symbolized the contradictions of the overextended U.S. military empire. He shared the neocon ambition to overthrow half a dozen governments and was infatuated with high-technology warfare; thus he spurned the Powell Doctrine that the United States should invade foreign nations only with overwhelming force. Rumsfeld tried to show that the United States could replace regimes in the Middle East without using more than 150,000 troops, and he had a vision of how to sustain global military dominance without instituting a draft.

For six years Rumsfeld pursued a plan called "military transformation" that globalized the military reach of the United States. He seeded the military with officials who shared his vision of a high-tech empire relying heavily on air power and rapid force projection. Dividing the globe among regional combatant commanders, he gave new responsibilities and financing to specialized commands, shifted regional war-fighting plans away from Cold War bases in Europe, and obtained easier access to the Middle East and Central Asia. He engineered a massive upgrade of the navy, heightening its already stupendous overkill capacity by investing in the DDX next-generation destroyer, the Virginia Class attack submarine, the Littoral Combat Ship, and the F-35 fighter-bomber. He also launched a high-tech army program called Future Combat Systems, an integrated structure of air and ground vehicles that communicate with each other and other units through a global military network.

The Future Combat Systems program includes unattended ground sensors and munitions; an intelligent munitions system; four classes of unmanned aerial vehicles organic to platoon, company, battalion, and Modular Force echelons; three classes of unmanned ground vehicles; an armed robotic vehicle; eight manned ground vehicles; a mounted combat system; and ten other systems acting as a unified combat force. The army describes it as the "core" of its mission to strike any region of the world quickly and powerfully. One of the program's boosters, GlobalSecurity.org, describes it more vividly as a revolutionary "leap ahead" system and the "centerpiece" of the next army: "lightweight, overwhelmingly lethal, strategically deployable, and self-sustaining." The first phase of the program, covering one-third of the army's present force, will cost $160 billion; $4 billion for it was allocated in 2007.

To the same end, Pentagon budgets are getting "blacker," to use the defense and intelligence jargon. Over 20 percent of the Pentagon's acquisition budget in 2008 is devoted to secret, classified programs, a return to the Cold War level of classified spending. Impending technologies such as warhead-like bullets and neurobiological signature-tracking satellites will give lethal new weapons to covert warriors, evading the politics of war. To the extent that the United States handles its global management problems with Special Forces and the CIA's military wing, it avoids having to deal with domestic politics and the U.N. Security Council. In recent years the CIA has become "greener" (increasing its uniformed military wing), and Special Forces have become "blacker" (emphasizing super-clandestine operations).

A further variation on this trend is the Pentagon's commitment to programs that could lead to the development of dual-use space weapons. The United States had no formal policy on new military missions in outer space until October 2006, when it announced a stunningly imperial one. On October 13, 2006, President Bush signed a National Space Policy that ruled out any future arms-control agreements that might limit U.S. operations in space. The new policy, which was vetted quietly in Congress, asserted that the United States has a right to deny access to space to any nation that the U.S. government deems to be "hostile to U.S. interests."

That is the Monroe Doctrine applied to outer space. There are no codes of conduct about how military missions in outer space would be conducted, nor any rules about how space weapons would be operated. The Bush administration contends that since there is no space arms race, there is no need of an arms control agreement in this area. Congress has never voted on, nor even debated, whether it wants to invest in space weapons. But the Bush administration has quietly funded programs that will create space weapon technologies.

The neoconservative vision of global empire trades on exceptionalist self-understandings permeating U.S. American history: God's New Israel, the City on a Hill, Manifest Destiny, the Redeemer Nation, Pax Americana, the Leader of the Free World. It offers a vision of what the United States should do with its unrivaled power. In its most rhetorically seductive versions it conflates the expansion of U.S. power with the dream of global democracy, as in President Bush's second inaugural address.

In other words, neoconservatism is merely an explicit, think-tank version of U.S. supremacism, one that defends the nation's routine practices of empire. Since the end of the Cold War, neoconservatism has been defined by its doctrine of "full-spectrum dominance," yet this doctrine is not unique to neoconservatives. It was a staple of defense industry and Pentagon literature before George W. Bush took office. The Joint Chiefs of Staff, in their *Joint Vision* statements of 1996 and 2000, declared that the United States is committed to sustaining full-spectrum dominance on a global scale as a primary military policy. *Joint Vision 2020,* issued on May 30, 2000, put it this way: "The overall goal of the transformation described in this document is the creation of a force that is dominant across the full spectrum of military operations—persuasive in peace, decisive in war, preeminent in any form of conflict. . . . Full spectrum dominance [is] the ability of U.S. forces, operating unilaterally or in combination with multinational and interagency partners, to defeat any adversary and control any situation across the full range of military options."

That statement, issued during the Clinton administration, put it as plainly as possible. For eight years, neoconservatives railed against President Clinton for wasting America's dominance. They wanted a huge military expansion and what they called "creative destruction" in the Middle East. When President Bush committed the United States to perpetual war, he and the neocons invoked the national myth that the United States invades only to liberate. This presumption is longstanding in U.S. history; it was a staple of July Fourth orations by the late nineteenth century. Until very recently, most U.S. Americans truly believed that their armed forces should be welcomed whenever they invade another country.

U.S. Americans today are absorbing contrary evidence. The United States needs a peace movement that stresses international cooperation, alternatives to war and militarism, and building new structures of collective security. The case for a stronger international community has a realistic basis, that the benefits of multilateral cooperation outweigh the costs and risks of not working together. A superpower that insists on absolute security for itself makes all other nations insecure. All parties are better off when the most powerful nations agree not to do everything that is in their power and nations work together to create new forms of collective security. In an increasingly interdependent world, nation-states have to cooperate with each other to address security issues that transcend national boundaries.

Increasingly U.S. citizens are awakening from the toxic combination of bad theology and bad politics that prevailed in the years following September 11, 2001. U.S. Americans were told that God is on their side, an "axis of evil" had to be overthrown, and the nation had a mission, as President Bush put it at the National Cathedral service, to "rid the world of evil." In good theology it is understood that God does not take sides with nations; there are always bad leaders to be coped with and contained; nations are too sinful and power-oriented to be instruments of redemption; and redemption from evil is God's business. The response of any Christian or other religious tradition to world politics must feature a strong presumption against war and a predisposition to view the world from the perspectives of the poor, the excluded, and the vulnerable. In biblical teaching, the test of ethical action is how it affects the struggles of oppressed and excluded people. Christianity must be a movement that shows the peaceable and justice-making way of Christ, bridging the moral chasm between the Christian historical record and the way of Jesus.

For me the normative gospel ethic of peacemaking, loving one's enemies, and what Jesus called the "weightier matters of the law"—justice and mercy—is integrative and contextual. It interrogates the ethics of prevention and defense on a case-by-case basis, and it has a place for humanitarian intervention. At the same time, the presumption against war must be very strong for an ethic to be Christian, and it must see the face of Christ in the faces of the world's disinherited.

For months leading up to the Iraq War, the Vatican, the World Council of Churches, and many other religious communities pleaded against invading Iraq. Pope John Paul II declared that the future of humanity depended on the courage of the earth's peoples and their leaders to reject "the logic of war." The Vatican mouthpiece *Civilta Cattolica* described the war as "a wound and a humiliation for the entire Islamic world" that was bound to fuel acts of revenge for many years to come. Many denominations and ecumenical organizations cited the gospel ethic of sacrificial love and the scriptural command not to kill. Virtually all of them began with the gospel presumption against war and went on to emphasize international law, international cooperation, collective security, and real-world consequences. The church has not lacked official statements against a war that did not come remotely close to being a last resort. The church has lacked, however, the mobilization of antiwar conviction that makes a difference.

Nearly forty years ago, Senator William Fulbright warned that the United States was well on its way to becoming an empire that exercised power for its own sake, projected to the limit of its capacity and beyond, filling every vacuum and extending U.S. American force to the farthest reaches of the earth. As the power grows, he warned, it becomes an end in itself, separated from its initial motives (all the while denying it), governed by its own mystique, projecting power merely because we have it.

If the United States had responded to 9/11 by sending NATO forces and Army Rangers after Al-Qaeda, rebuilding Afghanistan, and building new networks of collective security against terrorism and rogue states, it would have gained the world's gratitude. Instead it took an imperial course that caused an explosion of anti-Americanism throughout the world, a torrent of bitter feeling that has not abated. We need a peace movement that prevents the next unilateral war of choice from occurring, one that says: "I don't want my country, the country that I love, fighting wars of aggression. I don't want my country to spurn the hard work of collective security. I don't want my country to be dragged into wars that don't come remotely close to being a last resort, inflaming resentments that will last for centuries."

QUESTIONS FOR DISCUSSION

1. If the United States needs a larger and stronger peace movement, what local and national organizations might one join to help build one?
2. If the church needs to bridge the historical chasm between much of the Christian record and the way of Jesus, where does that work begin within the Christian community?
3. Most of the time U.S. American Christians try to minimize the tensions between following Christ and supporting U.S. military policies. In cases where Christians in the United States oppose a particular U.S. policy, we usually say that the policy does not really express or represent a genuine national interest. Describe a situation, however, where the two things really do conflict: a policy promotes a genuine national security or economic interest in clear conflict with a Christian norm. How should the Christian community respond to such a situation?

RESOURCES

Bellah, Robert. "Righteous Empire: Imperialism, American-style." *The Christian Century* 120 (March 8, 2003): 20–25.

Dorrien, Gary. "Grand Illusion: The Costs of War and Empire." *The Christian Century* 123 (December 26, 2006): 26–29.

———. *Imperial Design: Neoconservatism and the New Pax Americana.* New York: Routledge, 2004.

Wallis, Jim. "Dangerous Religion: George W. Bush's Theology of Empire." *Sojourners,* September/October 2003.

Web Sites

Center for Defense Information, http://www.cdi.org.

Global Security.org, http://www.globalsecurity.org.

National Defense Authorization Bill for 2008, http://armed-services.senate.gov/press.htm.

NOTES

1. Parts of this chapter are adapted from Gary Dorrien, *Imperial Designs: Neoconservatism and the New Pax Americana* (New York: Routledge, 2004), and Dorrien, "Grand Illusion: The Costs of War and Empire," *Christian Century,* December 26, 2006.
2. See "The Statement of Principles," http://www.newamericancentury.org/statementofprinciples.htm.
3. See "Rebuilding America's Defenses: Strategy, Forces, and Resources for a New Century." Available online at http://www.newamericancentury.org/RebuildingAmericasDefenses.pdf.

Chapter 12

For Funding Our Values

REBECCA TODD PETERS

When most of us remember John F. Kennedy's words, "Ask not what your country can do for you, ask what you can do for your country," we don't think about paying taxes. Yet the practice of giving a portion of one's income or wealth to support government expenses and services is a practice as old as civilization itself. Governments perform certain tasks that benefit the whole community, usually tasks that are viewed as important to the health, safety, and well-being of their citizens. These expenses must be paid for somehow, and the privilege of self-governance in a democracy comes with the responsibility of contributing financially to support the common good. While everyone within the U.S. political sphere can agree that we need to pay taxes of some sort, opinions about the appropriate role of government in social and business concerns vary significantly, as do opinions about where and how taxes should be levied.

Many people resist what they consider to be a high rate of taxation in the United States because they subscribe to the prevailing cultural attitude that they are "entitled" to their profits and wages. While it is certainly true that individuals deserve to be compensated for their labor, this attitude does not take into consideration larger questions and concerns that situate each individual wage earner and their dependents within a larger social framework. For instance, this attitude ignores the vast discrepancies between the salaries and wages of various workers in our society—most of whom work very hard at their jobs. It also supports a U.S. mythology of rugged individualism that often blinds people from recognizing that they did not get where they are entirely on their own. This attitude also ignores the many and varied ways in which we all benefit from goods and services provided by the federal government that promote our common good as a society. Paying taxes is a direct recognition of the important role that communities play in caring for one another in good times and in hard times.

The idea of entitlement used to be associated with the types of programs that worked toward the task assigned to us by the Preamble of the Constitution, namely to "promote the general welfare." People used to consider these kinds of programs (welfare, food stamps, Social Security, Medicare, Medicaid, disability, unemployment) necessary to the healthy functioning of society. Indeed, it was widely recognized that people were "entitled" to these benefits as an affirmation of the common humanity that we all share. Backlash against entitlement programs in recent years has given the impression that a large portion of our federal tax dollars goes to fund these programs. Many Americans would be surprised to know that out of every tax dollar roughly twenty-nine cents goes to the military and nineteen cents goes for interest on the national debt. That's half of our tax dollars right there. Out of the remaining fifty cents, four cents goes for education, two cents each go to housing and the environment, three cents to nutrition, and job training gets only one-third of a penny![1] Clearly the support that we, as a society, are giving to the "least of these" in our midst pales in comparison to the amount of our federal tax dollars that are being spent on war, defense, and debt.

As Christians who are concerned about the health and well-being of our communities, the global human community at large, and the life and health of all of God's creation, when it comes to thinking about issues of taxes and federal spending, the question is: does our national budget reflect the values that are truly important to progressive Christians? As we think about taxes, tax policy, and federal spending, we must ask ourselves what we value most. If we value safe and healthy communities, clean rivers and streams, and literacy and job training for our citizens, then we need budget priorities that reflect these issues.

The biblical mandate of social justice that echoes throughout both Testaments is clear in its instructions that humankind will be measured by our attention, care, and concern for the "least of these" in our midst. Currently, the quarter of the world's population who live in the developed world account for 86 percent of total private consumption, while three-quarters of the world must make do with the other 14 percent. In 2004 in the United States, the wealthiest 1 percent of the population held over 33 percent of the nation's private wealth. Wealth has not been this concentrated in our country since 1929, when the wealthiest 1 percent had 35 percent of all private wealth.[2] Patterns of wealth and poverty are neither natural nor inevitable, but rather a result of economic and public policies that function to allow for the concentration or the sharing of wealth. As inequality continues to increase within our own country and between people of the first world and people in the two-thirds world, it becomes increasingly necessary to think about our social obligations to others in the twenty-first century.

HISTORY OF TAXATION IN THE UNITED STATES

Just as certainly as taxes are an essential foundation of democracy, disagreement and protest about taxes are also foundational aspects of our history and experience of taxes in the United States. The Boston Tea Party was a protest against unfairly administered taxes; early colonists objected to the fact that they were required to pay taxes to the British government but were not allowed any representation in Parliament. In 1789, the Constitution gave the newly formed federal government the power to "lay and collect taxes, duties, imposts, and excises, pay the Debts and provide for the common Defense and general Welfare of the United States."[3] Congress raised money for many years through the use of tariffs and excise taxes to repay the debt from the Revolutionary War and to cover necessary expenses of the growing country.

With the notable exception of the current war in Iraq, taxes have always been raised as a means of paying for war. The outbreak of the Civil War saw Congress pass the Revenue Act of 1861, which instituted the first income tax in the United States. This was repealed soon after the war ended, and not until the Sixteenth Amendment was passed in 1913 did the country shift to relying primarily on direct taxes of income and wealth. The first tax rates for this income tax ranged from 1 to 7 percent on incomes over five hundred thousand dollars (only 1 percent of the population). Expenses from World War I increased the tax rates to 6 percent on the lower end and 77 percent at the top.[4] Originally promoted as a "class" tax on "surplus" income, only 5 percent of the population actually paid income taxes in 1918; even so, income tax revenue paid for one-third of the war expenses.[5]

While tax rates fell after the end of the war, the Depression once again prompted Congress to raise taxes in order to reduce rising budget deficits. The Social Security Act of 1935 introduced a new category of taxes that was intended as a social safety net program to provide unemployment benefits to people who were out of work as well as public aid for disability, the elderly, and other marginalized people in society. World War II again brought increased need for federal revenue to support the war effort, and tax rates increased at the lower end of the tax scale to 23 percent and rose to 94 percent on incomes over $1 million. As the tax rates increased, the requirement to pay them inched down to include more and more workers at the middle and lower end of the pay scale. By the end of WWII the number of people paying federal income taxes had grown from 4 million in 1939 to 43 million in 1945.[6]

From 1947 to 1979, economic prosperity was shared broadly across the country as real family income grew significantly at every income level of U.S. society. Increased federal revenues in the 1950s allowed Congress to expand public services and social systems that promoted affordable education, home ownership, decent jobs (through public works programs), a national highway system, and employment and training programs.[7] However, not all U.S. citizens were able to take advantage of the support systems provided by the federal government. Institutionalized racism often prevented minority groups from accessing these public services and social supports as practices such as redlining and Jim Crow laws prevented blacks from accessing home ownership and segregated public facilities. Even with the increasing prosperity of the 1950s, Census data from 1959 shows that the poverty rate was 18.5 percent.[8]

In the 1960s, Lyndon Johnson declared a "War on Poverty," and his administration oversaw the development and expansion of a host of federal programs that were intended to promote what Johnson referred to as the Great Society. These programs included Medicaid and Medicare, Head Start, Food Stamps, Job Corps, and other programs that supported housing, health, mental health, and education. Many of these programs, along with Social Security and unemployment, are referred to as a "social safety net." They are meant to catch people who fall through the cracks of our society and are intended to help them get back on their feet. While there will always be a handful of people who abuse these benefits, studies have shown that most people use programs exactly as they were intended as short-term support to help them get back on their feet. By the late 1970s, there was increasing dissatisfaction with the federal tax system as Congress increased tax breaks for businesses and wealthy individuals while increasing the tax rates of the middle class. High inflation during this period also eroded the real value of traditional middle-class tax exemptions.[9]

The election of Ronald Reagan in 1980 saw a significant shift in political and economic philosophy as the promotion of the new ideology of Reaganomics was predicated on reducing taxes and the size of government. The supply-side economics that lay at the heart of Reaganomics was based on the belief that economic growth required increased savings and investment by wealthy individuals and corporations and a reduced governmental role in business. Practically, this approach has meant an increasing reduction of taxes on the wealthiest members of society and an increasing tax burden on the middle class. Between 1948 and 1999, the effective tax rate of the top 1 percent of households dropped 57 percent while that of median-income households almost quadrupled.[10]

The erosion of corporate tax revenues parallels the shift in declining tax rates of the wealthy over the last half century. Persuaded by the argument that lower tax burdens are necessary to keep businesses in the United States competitive, revenues from corporate taxes now make up only about 10 percent of federal revenues as compared with 20 to 30 percent of federal revenue from the 1940s through the 1960s.[11] "In 2000, an estimated 94 percent of U.S. corporations and 89 percent of foreign corporations doing business in the United States paid less than 5 percent of their total incomes in taxes."[12]

VALUING TAXES

Revenue from taxes enables federal, state, and local governments to offer a variety of essential public services that contribute to the common good of society, such as police and fire protection, education, criminal justice, the military, social services, parks, and transportation. Some public services—libraries, parks, and highways, for example—are available for use by all members of society. Other government-provided services, like education, prisons, and social services, are generally regarded as a public responsibility that contributes to the overall well-being of society. Some government-funded programs like research, drug rehabilitation, and job training are viewed as investments in future productivity and human resources.[13]

While taxes are a necessary practice for raising public funds, there is wide variation when it comes to what can be taxed and who will pay them. Taxes are traditionally levied on goods and services, income, property, and wealth, and are paid by individual citizens and by businesses and corporations. Ultimately, decisions about what and who to tax are a reflection of the values of society. What do we tax? At what rate? How should the tax burden be divided among members of a society? There are three basic philosophical approaches to taxation: regressive, proportional, and progressive.

Regressive Taxes

Requiring all citizens to pay equal monetary payments is the most basic way of approaching the goal of equity in taxation.[14] The underlying principle is that if everyone benefits equally from the public services provided by the government—fire, police, defense, education, and so on—then everyone should contribute equally to fund them. Sales taxes are an example of a tax policy based on the assumption that everyone should pay the same amount, as all people who purchase these goods and services pay the same tax.

From an abstract philosophical perspective, the idea of sharing the tax responsibility equally has a certain egalitarian appeal. However, within a society where there is economic inequality, the poor end up paying a much greater proportion of their income in taxes. For example, imagine that two people each bought a new car for twenty thousand dollars with a sales tax of 5 percent. The first person is a schoolteacher who makes thirty thousand dollars a year and the second person is a lawyer who makes three hundred thousand dollars a year. While each of them would owe the same sales tax of one thousand dollars, the effective sales tax rate (tax as a percentage of income) for the teacher would be 3.3 percent of her salary, while the rate for the lawyer would be .003 percent of her salary. While billed as "equal," in reality these taxes take a larger proportion of the salary of lower-income groups than from higher-income groups. In effect, the less you earn, the higher your tax rate. Consequently, these types of taxes are known as "regressive" taxes.

Proportional Taxes

One way to address the inequality of regressive taxes is to require everyone to pay the same proportion of their income. In this case the principle of equality is still valued, but the tax system allows for differences in economic circumstances and taxes each person proportionate to his or her income and wealth. This is the philosophy behind the recommendation that a flat tax or standard tax rate be used to collect income taxes. Theoretically, within a flat tax system everyone would pay a flat rate or a certain percentage of their income in taxes. Recent proposals for flat tax plans in the United States range from 15 to 17 percent; however, the real impact of flat tax plans are often hidden in proposals for exemptions that benefit the wealthy. Here, the word "proportional" refers to the tax rate in proportion to one's income.

A second way that the term "proportional" is used in tax debates is to refer to a standardized tax rate that applies to the value or cost of the taxed item. Examples of this type of proportional tax include sales and property taxes, which are generally set at a standard rate across all income levels. However, as we saw in the example of the schoolteacher and the lawyer above, sales and property taxes are proportional and regressive in nature because the overall tax burden ends up being more severe for people in lower income brackets than for people in higher income brackets when examined as a proportion of one's total income.

Progressive Taxes

While tax policy in the United States has been regressing over the last thirty years as evidenced by the tax cuts for the wealthy we saw earlier, the nation has maintained a progressive tax structure for close to the last one hundred years, ever since a federal income tax policy was first initiated. Generally speaking, regressive and proportional taxes have been recognized as systems that place an undue burden on lower- and middle-income taxpayers who generally have less disposable income than more affluent citizens. Since greater proportions of the incomes of lower- and middle-class wage earners are used to meet their basic needs of food, shelter, and clothing with modest amounts left over for discretionary purchases, the taxes that they do pay have a more immediate effect on their personal well-being than for more wealthy citizens. A graduated or progressive tax structure means that tax rates increase as one's ability to pay increases; therefore, people with higher incomes pay higher rates of taxes. A progressive tax policy is based on the principle that those who have more are able to pay more.

This description of various approaches to taxation helps us to see some of the impacts, burdens, and values implicit in tax policy, but it does not address the heart of the question of how progressive Christians should approach the issue of taxation. Let us now turn to the task of thinking about the values that we share as Christians for society and how those values might inform our tax policy.

CHRISTIAN ETHICS AND TAX POLICY

The basic foundation of the social fabric that holds Christian life together is the idea of covenant. Within biblical theology, a covenant is a binding agreement between two parties that is usually initiated by God with individuals (Noah, Abraham, David) or with groups (covenant with creation after the flood, Sinai covenant made with the Hebrew people). The making of a covenant signifies something more important than a simple contractual agreement between two parties. It signifies the initiation and development of a binding social relationship between God and the covenant people that is marked by loyalty and a concern for mutual well-being and right relationships between the members of the covenant community, even when the members are unfaithful or break the covenant.[15] The covenant relationship between God and Israel formed the foundation for moral action and accountability for the Hebrew people, and Christians understand the actions and teachings of Jesus as a continuation of the covenant relationship between God and God's people.

When God adopts Israel into a covenant relationship through the Sinai covenant, God stipulates a clear set of covenant obligations that the Hebrew people are to follow in order to stay in right relation with God. These covenant obligations include explicit instructions for community relationships and responsibilities that are intended to create communities and social relationships that are just. However, we often hear more about Israel's covenant obligations in relation to the breaking of the covenant than in its fulfillment.

The prophets rightly understood that covenant righteousness formed the foundation of the social community within Israel, and the bulk of their task was to call the people of God to account for breaking their covenant promises and obligations. When the breach of these covenant responsibilities affects the life of the community and results in the damaging of social relationships and responsibilities, it is often referred to as social injustice. Repeatedly we hear the prophets cry out in judgment against the people for neglecting their covenant responsibilities. Isaiah cries out to the people to "cease to do evil, learn to do good; seek justice, rescue the oppressed, defend the orphan, plead for the widow" (Isa. 1:16–17). Micah condemns the people because "they covet fields, and seize them; houses, and take them away; they oppress householder and house, people and their inheritance" (Mic. 2:2). But the prophets' purpose is not simply condemnation; the prophets understand that the covenant relationship means that God will not give up on the people, but desires the renewal of justice and the reestablishment of a society and a people whose lives are again marked by covenant faithfulness.

The images of covenant relationship and justice offer progressive Christians a strong foundation for developing a theological basis for decisions about tax policy. Remembering our own covenant relationship with God, we are called to think about our covenant responsibilities to each other as Christians in community; to the earth and all our neighbors, near and far; and to God. As we consider the implications of covenant and justice for our own social relationships, it is important to think about how these values can inform our thinking about taxation and federal spending. As the wealthiest country in the world, it is our own moral failure that we continue to structure our society in ways that allow for almost 17 percent of our population to live in poverty or near-poverty circumstances.[16] Like the prophets from our past, the recent statements on economic globalization from our ecumenical partners in the World Council of Churches and the World Alliance of Reformed Churches[17] are calling us to account for living lives of comfort, and even luxury, while our neighbors in the two-thirds world die of starvation, pollution, disease, and war.

While no single plan for restructuring taxes can address the many problems that we face, we can adopt several specific tax policies that would reflect a deeper commitment to covenant and justice. Some suggestions to consider:

- Repeal the tax cuts implemented by the Bush administration and shore up the historical progressive nature of the U.S. tax system.
- Require businesses and transnational corporations to make reasonable contributions to the federal treasury as a reflection of the benefits that they receive from operating in the United States.
- Implement a tax, like the Tobin tax,[18] on currency trading as a way to curtail currency speculation that often has a destabilizing effect on fragile economies, and use the money to fund international justice initiatives that alleviate poverty and promote health and well-being.
- Maintain support for the estate tax, which taxes estates larger than $2 million and only affects the estates of one-half of 1 percent of deceased persons.

As the chapters in this book have demonstrated, public policies that relate to public goods like education, housing, families, social security, criminal justice, drugs, wages, immigration, healthcare, the environment, and the military all have the potential for helping to shape a more just domestic society. Ultimately, a more just domestic society will also mean that United States will become a more just global partner and ally. With the notable exception of the military, every other social concern raised in this book is seriously underfunded. While money is not a panacea, adequately attending to the social problems in our country in creative and innovative ways requires increased federal revenue, as well as a reprioritization of how our federal tax dollars are spent.

QUESTIONS FOR DISCUSSION

1. Individually, or as a group, make a list of all of the government services or supports that have impacted your life over the last week. Discuss the value of these services for your community, for the nation. What would the impact on the common good be if people were forced to pay for these services individually?
2. Brainstorm a list of covenant obligations that you consider to be crucial to your own identity as Christians in community. What insight do your covenant obligations to God and to others offer for thinking about how to care for "the least of these" in our midst—those in the United States and those in other countries? How might this relate to thinking about taxes and tax policy?
3. Many candidates for public office try to lure voters by promising they won't raise taxes, a political strategy that often wins votes. How does the idea of covenant and our responsibility to community reframe our understanding of taxes and the way taxes function in our society?

RESOURCES

Book

Abromovitz, Mimi, and Sandra Morgen with the National Council for Research. *Taxes Are a Woman's Issue: Reframing the Debate*. New York: Feminist Press, 2006.
Giecek, Tamara Sober. *Teaching Economics as If People Mattered*. Boston: Dollars and Sense, 2007.
Gates, William H., and Chuck Collins. *Why America Should Tax Accumulated Fortunes*. Boston: Beacon Press, 2003.

Web Sites

National Priorities Project, http://nationalpriorities.org.
Tax Policy Center, http://www.taxpolicycenter.org.
UN Millennium Development Goals, http://www.un.org/millenniumgoals.

NOTES

1. Statistics on federal tax spending come from the National Priorities Project and are based on the 2005 federal budget of the U.S. government. See http://nationalpriorities.org/auxiliary/interactivetaxchart/taxchart.html?T1=10 (accessed September 26, 2007).
2. Tamara Sober Giecek with United for a Fair Economy, *Teaching Economics as If People Mattered* (Boston: United for a Fair Economy, 2007), 161.
3. "History of the U.S. Tax System: Fact Sheet," http://www.treas.gov/education/fact-sheets/taxes/ustax.shtml (accessed September 23, 2007).
4. Ibid.
5. Ibid.
6. Ibid.
7. Mimi Abromovitz and Sandra Morgen with the National Council for Research, *Taxes Are a Woman's Issue: Reframing the Debate* (New York: Feminist Press, 2006), 69.
8. Elenora Giddings Ivory, "Ask the Director," *Washington Report*, March/April 2005, http://www.pcusa.org/washington/march-april05.htm#3 (accessed September 26, 2007).
9. Abromovitz and Morgen, *Taxes Are a Woman's Issue*, 69–70.
10. Ibid., 71.
11. The Budget for the Fiscal Year 2007, Historical Tables, "Table 2.2—Percentage Composition of Receipts by Source: 1934–2011," 31–32, http://www.whitehouse.gov/omb/budget/fy2007/pdf/hist.pdf (accessed September 24, 2007).
12. Abromovitz and Morgen, *Taxes Are a Woman's Issue*, 75.
13. Internal Revenue Service, "Lesson One: Why Pay Taxes?" http://www.irs.gov/app/understandingTaxes/jsp/whys/lp/IWT1L1lp.jsp (accessed September 25, 2007).
14. Ronald M. Green, "Ethics and Taxation: A Theoretical Framework," *Journal of Religious Ethics* 12 (Fall 1984): 146–61.
15. Joseph L. Allen, "Covenant," in *The Westminster Dictionary of Christian Ethics*, ed. James F. Childress and John Macquarrie (Philadelphia: Westminster Press, 1986).
16. U.S. Census Bureau Data, http://www.census.gov/hhes/www/poverty/poverty06/table4.pdf (accessed September 26, 2007).
17. See appendixes 3 and 4 for the full text of these statements.
18. The Tobin tax is a suggested tax of 0.1 to 0.25 percent of the trade of all currencies across borders. The tax was first proposed by economist James Tobin as a way to curtail potentially damaging short-term speculation in currency markets.

Appendix 1

Advocacy Advice

Our lawmakers' votes are influenced by their personal views, their party's positions, the advice of staff and friends, and lobbyists. But the single most important influence is constituent opinion. Members of Congress rely on the letters, phone calls, e-mails, faxes, and visits they receive to gauge how the voters in their district are thinking. Through effective contacts with decision makers, we can lift up the church's vision of a just and compassionate society. What follows is advice on how to advocate effectively for policy changes and reforms with your members of Congress.[1]

LETTER WRITING

Many people feel that letters, faxes, and e-mails don't make a difference. But a well-written, well-informed, personal letter from a voter in the lawmaker's district can indeed have an influence.

Your letter works two ways. First, it educates. Members of Congress must take positions on hundreds of issues; typically, they are well informed about only a few of them. They depend heavily on aides for summaries of information. Thought-provoking letters may shape the thinking of aides and thereby influence a member of Congress.

Second, it persuades. Aides keep a running tally of letters, faxes, and e-mails received for and against a given position. Although Congresspersons do not usually read individual correspondence, they do receive mail counts, by subject and attitude. Sometimes just a few faxes, e-mails, or letters are received on a given subject, and in that case even one can be important.

Tips for Writing

- Be brief. Express your opinion in a few paragraphs or even a few sentences, making clear what you are asking the lawmaker to do. Long, complicated communications are unlikely to be read all the way through by the Congressperson's busy staff.
- It's fine to send along one or two pieces of supporting material, such as an article from a local paper in the congressional district.
- If sending a letter, a neatly handwritten note is best. Otherwise, type. Check your spelling.
- State your own views in your own words. Form letters or postcards that appear generated by a mail campaign receive less attention than a personal note.
- Be positive and polite. If possible, begin by thanking the legislator for a past vote or action of which you approved.
- Address only one issue in a fax, e-mail, or letter. If possible, give the bill number and/or title. Let the lawmaker know precisely what you'd like him or her to do (for example, co-sponsor a bill, oppose or support certain amendments, vote for or against the bill when it comes to the floor).
- Draw on personal or local experience whenever possible to support your stand. Mention conditions or events in the legislator's district that relate to the legislation you're discussing.
- Ask questions. Thoughtful inquiries may prompt the lawmaker's staff to look into the issue more deeply in order to answer you.
- Time and target your contact. Early in the session, a note raising an issue in general terms may be appropriate. Later, time your faxes and e-mails to the progress of specific bills. Write to committee members soon after a bill has been referred to their committee. When the bill is sent to the floor of either chamber, write to your representative or senators.
- Be sure to put your return address and e-mail address on any communication.
- Be prepared for a less-than-satisfying response. Lawmakers' offices often send the same letter in reply to all constituents who write on a

given topic, usually amounting to little more than a bland restatement of the lawmaker's views. This does not mean your effort had no impact. Especially if many comments were received on the same topic, it may even have prodded the lawmaker to rethink his or her position or vote. Watch to see what action is taken on the issue you are concerned about, then follow up. If you approve, write a short note of thanks. If you disapprove, let the legislator know you are disappointed and restate your expectations.

E-MAIL AND FAX

Fax and e-mail have gained popularity as ways to communicate with Congress, particularly since the 2001 anthrax attacks. Sending a fax gets your message there fast—as fast as a phone call—and yet provides a written record of the communication. Though some offices do not give out their fax number publicly, in most cases fax is a direct and valid way to communicate.

Members of Congress have public e-mail boxes to which constituents can send correspondence. Certain House and Senate committees also have them. E-mails now get as much attention as do letters, faxes, or phone calls. They are easy to send—so easy that the legislator's e-mail box may be crowded with junk mail. If you send an e-mail message, include your postal mail address to show that you are in his or her district and to enable the office to send you a reply.

VISITING YOUR LEGISLATORS

You can arrange a visit to a lawmaker's local or Washington office. Locally, you should be able to meet with the member of Congress when he or she is in the home district during a congressional recess. For maximum impact, organize a delegation that includes representatives of several groups in your community. In Washington, your interview will most likely be with an aide on the lawmaker's staff. This does not mean that the meeting is less effective. Aides brief their member of Congress on the issues. They write the speeches, and in many cases recommend how the senator or representative should vote. To schedule a visit, write or phone ahead, preferably at least two weeks in advance. State the groups you represent, the issue you wish to discuss, how many people will attend, and your preferred dates for visiting. Confirm the date with a letter.

Plan ahead. Research in advance the current status of the legislation, the different sides of the argument, and the legislator's voting record and committee assignments. If several of you will be making the visit, have a strategy session.

Plan the points you will stress and who will take the lead; agree on questions you will ask and materials you will bring. Assume you will have only ten minutes to make your case. If you are given more time, you can expand the topic. When you begin a conversation with your legislator or an aide, introduce yourselves as constituents and mention any organizations that you represent. Briefly share your experience or credentials relevant to the issue you want to discuss. Comment on one of the lawmaker's past votes, thanking him or her, if possible, for a vote or action you favored.

State the purpose of your visit. Explain your position succinctly, and request specific actions that you want your legislator to take (e.g., co-sponsor a bill, vote for or against a measure in committee or on the floor). Ask what the lawmaker plans to do. Be persistent and polite. One person should take notes during the conversation, being sure to write down any commitments made by the legislator or aide. Afterward, send a letter thanking the member of Congress for the meeting. Briefly recap your position and your understanding of any commitments made during the meeting.

USING THE TELEPHONE

Telephoning your senator or representative is another way to communicate your opinion. If you call the home office, ask the staffer who takes your message to pass it on to the Washington office. A more effective approach is to call the Washington office directly and ask to speak with the legislative aide who deals with your issue. Or you can do both.

Prepare for the conversation in advance, jotting down the points you want to make. When you reach your listener, identify yourself as a constituent. Be pleasant and come to the point quickly. Ask how the lawmaker intends to vote on the issue, and state exactly what you want him or her to do.

Telephoning is useful when time is short. It is especially effective just before an important vote. On the other hand, writing costs less and provides a written record. Writing also allows you to provide supporting material, such as an article or report.

To reach the Washington office of any member of Congress or any congressional committee, phone the Capitol switchboard: (202) 224-3121. Ask by name for the office you want. You can also find out a senator's or representative's direct phone or fax number in Washington by calling his or her local office.

To express your opinion of an administration action, phone the White House comment line, (202) 456-1111, or fax the White House at (202) 456-2461.

Although individual messages are not relayed to the president, the White House pays attention to the volume of public response—for and against—especially following a major presidential speech or action.

LETTERS TO THE EDITOR AND OP-EDS

Letters to the editor are among the most widely read features of newspapers. A metropolitan daily may have 1 million to 2 million readers. Small-town papers are widely read and influential in their areas. When your letter appears on the editorial page, you probably have the largest audience you will ever address. Moreover, members of Congress normally read the newspaper from their district to keep tabs on issues of concern to their constituents. To give your letter the best chance of publication:

- Type the letter, double-spaced, on only one side of the paper.
- Keep it short, less than two pages.
- Deal with only one topic. It should be timely and newsworthy. If possible, refer to a news item, editorial, or letter that has appeared recently in the paper you are writing to.
- Express your thoughts clearly and concisely. A well-written letter is more likely to be published.
- Supply facts that may have been omitted or slanted in presentation of the news or editorials. You can render a service to the public by presenting views that may ordinarily be given little or no attention by the press. Avoid a hostile or sarcastic tone.
- Use a relevant personal experience to illustrate a point. If your background gives you special expertise on a subject, say so.
- Bring moral judgments to bear upon the issues. Appeal to readers' sense of justice and compassion. Challenge them to respond to the issue.
- Sign your name. Include your address and telephone number. In most cases only your name and city or town of residence will be published with the letter.

Opinion pieces (op-eds) are harder to get published than letters. In leading newspapers such as *The New York Times*, your chances of placing an op-ed are slim. Newspapers in mid-sized cities and towns offer greater possibilities. If you do get your letter into the paper, send a copy to your member of Congress.

An op-ed should be under 750 words (three double-spaced pages). It must be able to stand alone as a complete essay. Establish how your background gives you expertise on the subject. If your local paper's editorial position on a given issue is consistently at odds with what you believe is right, or if an important issue isn't getting covered in the paper, you may want to meet with the editors. This is most feasible if you can organize a small delegation (two or three people) that includes representatives of several groups in the community. The guidelines for visiting congressional offices also apply here, except that you are asking for more or different news coverage rather than a vote. Prepare for the meeting carefully. Bring a selection of background materials such as fact sheets and reports from identified and credible sources to leave with the editors, along with the telephone numbers of people who can be contacted for further information.

NOTE

1. This appendix is excerpted and adapted from a publication of the Washington Office of the Presbyterian Church (U.S.A.) titled, "How To Be an Effective Advocate . . . Making Our Voices Heard!"

Appendix 2

A Social Creed for the Twenty-first Century

We Churches of the United States have a message of hope for a fearful time. Just as the churches challenged the harshness of early-twentieth-century industrialization with a prophetic "Social Creed" in 1908, so in our era of globalization we offer a vision of a society that shares more and consumes less, seeks compassion over suspicion and equality over domination, and finds security in joined hands rather than massed arms. Inspired by Isaiah's vision of a "peaceable kingdom," we honor the dignity of every person and the intrinsic value of every creature and pray and work for the day when none "labor in vain or bear children for calamity" (Isa. 65:23). We do so as disciples of the One who came "that all may have life, and have it abundantly" (John 10:10), in solidarity with Christians and *with all who strive for justice* around the world.

In faith, responding to our Creator, we celebrate the full humanity of each woman, man, and child, all created in the divine image as individuals of infinite worth, by working for:

- Full civil, political, and economic rights for women and men of all races.

- Abolition of forced labor, human trafficking, and the exploitation of children.
- Employment for all, at a family-sustaining living wage, with equal pay for comparable work.
- The rights of workers to organize, and to share in workplace decisions and productivity growth.
- Protection from dangerous working conditions, with time and benefits to enable full family life.
- A system of criminal rehabilitation, based on restorative justice and end to the death penalty.

In the love incarnate in Jesus, despite the world's sufferings and evils, we honor the deep connections within our human family and seek to awaken a new spirit of community, by working for:

- Abatement of hunger and poverty, and enactment of policies benefiting the most vulnerable.
- High-quality public education for all and universal, affordable, and accessible healthcare.
- An effective program of social security during sickness, disability, and old age.
- Tax and budget policies that reduce disparities between rich and poor, strengthen democracy, and provide greater opportunity for everyone within the common good.
- Just immigration policies that protect family unity, safeguard workers' rights, require employer accountability, and foster international cooperation.
- Sustainable communities marked by affordable housing, access to good jobs, public transportation, and public safety.
- Public service as a high vocation, with real limits on the power of private interests in politics.

In hope sustained by the Holy Spirit, we pledge to be peacemakers in the world and stewards of God's good creation, by working for:

- Adoption of simpler lifestyles for those who have enough; grace over greed in economic life.
- Access for all to clean air and water and healthy food, through wise care of land and technology.
- Sustainable use of Earth's resources, promoting alternative energy sources and public transportation with binding convenants to reduce global warming and protect populations most affected.
- Equitable global trade and aid that protects local economies, cultures, and livelihoods.

- Peacemaking through multilateral diplomacy rather than unilateral force, the abolition of torture, strengthening the United Nations and the rule of international law.
- Nuclear disarmament and redirection of military spending to more peaceful and productive uses.
- Cooperation and dialogue for peace and environmental justice among the world's religions.

We—individual Christians and churches—commit ourselves to a culture of peace and freedom that embraces nonviolence, nurtures character, treasures the environment, and builds community, rooted in a spirituality of inner growth with outward action. We make this commitment together—as members of Christ's body, led by the one Spirit—trusting in the God who makes all things new.

Approved by the General Assembly of the National Council of Churches of Christ in the U.S.A., November 7, 2007.

Appendix 3

AGAPE Document (Alternative Globalization Addressing Peoples and Earth)

World Council of Churches

A CALL TO LOVE AND ACTION

Introduction

We, representatives of churches gathered at the ninth assembly of the World Council of Churches (WCC), emphasize that a world without poverty is not only possible but is in keeping with the grace of God for the world. This conviction builds on the rich tradition of ecumenical social thought and action, which is centred on God's option for the poor as an imperative of our faith. It captures the results of a seven-year global study process of the churches' responses to economic globalization with contributions from all regions of the world and involvement of a number of Christian world communions, particularly through the 2003 assembly of the Lutheran World Federation (LWF) and the 2004 general council of the World Alliance of Reformed Churches (WARC) (see Appendix 4). This process has examined the project of economic globalization that is led by the ideology of unfettered market forces and serves the dominant political and economic interests. The international financial institutions and the

World Trade Organization among other such institutions promote economic globalization. The participants in the AGAPE process shared their concerns about the growing inequality, the concentration of wealth and power in the hands of a few and the destruction of the earth—all aggravating the scandal of poverty in the South and increasingly in the North. In recent years the escalating role of political and military power have strongly surfaced. People all over the world experience the impact of imperial forms of power on their communities. Meeting in Porto Alegre, Brazil, the home of the World Social Forum (WSF), we are encouraged by the constructive and positive message of the movements gathering in the WSF that alternatives are possible. We affirm that we can and must make a difference by becoming transformative communities caring for people and the earth. We recognize that the divisions of the world are present among us. Since we are called to be one in Christ, we are called to be transformed by God's grace for the sake of all life on earth, overcoming the world's division. Challenged to monitor and transform economic globalization, we call ourselves to action as churches working alongside people of faith communities and movements.

AGAPE CALL—FOR LOVE AND ACTION

God, Creator, endowing your creation with integrity and human beings with dignity;

God, Redeemer and Liberator, freeing us from slavery and death;

God, Holy Spirit, transforming and energizing us.

Father, Son and Holy Spirit, let us witness to your love, life and transforming grace.

All: God, in your grace, transform the world.

We have become apathetic to suffering and injustice. Among us are many who suffer the consequences of economic globalization; women, abused and yet caring for life; children who are denied their rights; youth living in economic insecurity and unemployment; those labouring under exploitative conditions; the many caught in unjust trade relationships and debt slavery. There are people with disabilities and those living at the margins of society, people of colour often the first and most painfully hit by poverty, those pushed away and alienated from the land, the earth—battered, depleted and exploited. Denied of their sustenance, these people are often the most vulnerable to diseases such as HIV/AIDS. We confess that many of us have failed to respond in solidarity.

All: God, in your grace, transform the world.

We are tempted to give in to comfort and its empty promises when we ought to choose costly discipleship and change. We are driven to accept oppression and suffering as a given, when we should keep our hope and advocate for justice and liberation. We confess that many of us have failed to take a stand in our faith and act against economic injustice and its destructive consequences on people and the earth. We are tempted to give in to materialism and the reign of money. We play to the rules of greed and conform to political and military power when we should align ourselves with the poor and excluded people.

All: God, in your grace, transform the world.

God, we ask your forgiveness.

All: God, in your grace, transform the world.

God, let our economic structures be inspired by the rules of your household of life, governed by love, justice and grace.
Let us not be afraid of change, or to seek alternatives.
Let us work for justice by resisting destructive economic structures,
Proclaiming with hope the jubilee year of the Lord, the cancellation of debt, the release of the captives and rest for the land,
let us work for an agape economy of solidarity.

All: God, in your grace, transform the world.

God, you send us out,
to care for the earth and to share all what is necessary for life in community;
to resist and to denounce all that denies life,
to love our neighbours and to do what is just,
so that where there was death, there will be life.
We call each other to respond to your love for all people and for the earth in our own actions and in the witness and service of our churches;
to work for the eradication of poverty and the unconditional cancellation of debts;
to care for land, water, air—the entire web of life;
to build just and sustainable relationships with the earth.
In the world of labour, trade and finance to study and engage power in its different forms and manifestations, remembering that all power is accountable to you, God. God in your grace, help us to be agents of your transformation and to hear your call to act with courage.

All: Creator God, may the power of your grace transform us,
Christ, give us courage and hope to share our life with each other and the world,
Holy Spirit, empower us to work for justice for people and the earth.
God, in your grace, transform the world. Amen.

In the spirit of this uniting prayer, we challenge ourselves to have the courage to take action. The AGAPE call invites us to act together for transformation of economic injustice and to continue analyzing and reflecting on challenges of economic globalization and the link between wealth and poverty.

1. Poverty eradication

We recommit ourselves to work for the eradication of poverty and inequality through developing economies of solidarity and sustainable communities. We will hold our governments and the international institutions accountable to implement their commitments on poverty eradication and sustainability.

2. Trade

We recommit ourselves to work for justice in international trade relations through critical analyses on free trade and trade negotiations, and to collaborate closely with social movements in making those agreements just, equitable and democratic.

3. Finance

We recommit ourselves to campaign for responsible lending; unconditional debt cancellation and for the control and regulation of global financial markets. Investments should be redirected towards businesses that respect social and ecological justice, or in banks and institutions that do not engage in speculation, nor encourage tax evasion.

4. Sustainable use of land and natural resources

We recommit ourselves to engage in actions for sustainable and just patterns of extraction and use of natural resources, in solidarity with Indigenous peoples, who seek to protect their land, water and their communities. We recommit ourselves to challenge the excessive consumption of affluent societies so that they will shift towards self-restraint and simplicity in lifestyles.

5. Public goods and services

We recommit ourselves to join the global struggle against the imposed privatization of public goods and services; and to actively defend the rights of countries and peoples to define and manage their own commons. We recommit ourselves to support movements, groups and international initiatives defending vital elements of life such as bio-diversity, water and the atmosphere.

6. Life-giving agriculture

We recommit ourselves to work for land reforms in solidarity with landless agricultural labourers and small farm holders; to advocate in various ways for self-determination over food concerns; to oppose the production of genetically modified organisms (GMOs) as well as trade liberalization as the sole directive. We commit ourselves to promote ecological farming practices and to stand in solidarity with peasant communities.

7. Decent jobs, emancipated work and people's livelihoods

We commit ourselves to build alliances with social movements and trade unions that advocate decent jobs and just wages. We commit ourselves to advocate for those workers and bonded labourers who work under exploitative conditions and are deprived of their rights to form trade unions.

8. Churches and the power of empire

We recommit ourselves to reflect on the question of power and empire from a biblical and theological perspective, and take a firm faith stance against hegemonic powers because all power is accountable to God. We acknowledge that the process of transformation requires that we as churches make ourselves accountable to the victims of the project of economic globalization. Their voices and experiences must determine how we analyze and judge this project, in keeping with the gospel. This implies that we as churches from different regions make ourselves accountable to each other, and that those of us closer to the centres of power live out our first loyalty to our sisters and brothers who experience the negative impacts of global economic injustice every day of their lives. This AGAPE call is a prayer for strength to transform unjust economic structures. It will guide our reflections and actions in the next phase of the ecumenical journey. Our engagement will build on the findings, proposals and recommendations to the churches from the AGAPE process as outlined in the AGAPE background document.

Appendix 4

Accra Confession (Covenanting for Justice in the Economy and the Earth)

World Alliance of Reformed Churches

INTRODUCTION

1. In response to the urgent call of the Southern African constituency which met in Kitwe in 1995 and in recognition of the increasing urgency of global economic injustice and ecological destruction, the 23rd General Council (Debrecen, Hungary, 1997) invited the member churches of the World Alliance of Reformed Churches to enter into a process of "recognition, education, and confession (processus confessionis)". The churches reflected on the text of Isaiah 58.6, ". . . break the chains of oppression and the yoke of injustice, and let the oppressed go free," as they heard the cries of brothers and sisters around the world and witnessed God's gift of creation under threat.

2. Since then, nine member churches have committed themselves to a faith stance; some are in the process of covenanting; and others have studied the issues and come to a recognition of the depth of the crisis. Further, in partnership with the World Council of Churches, the Lutheran World Federation and regional ecumenical organizations, the World Alliance of Reformed Churches has engaged in consultations in all regions of the world, from Seoul/Bangkok (1999)

to Stony Point (2004). Additional consultations took place with churches from the South in Buenos Aires (2003) and with churches from South and North in London Colney (2004).

3. Gathered in Accra, Ghana, for the General Council of the World Alliance of Reformed Churches, we visited the slave dungeons of Elmina and Cape Coast where millions of Africans were commodified, sold and subjected to the horrors of repression and death. The cries of "never again" are put to the lie by the ongoing realities of human trafficking and the oppression of the global economic system.

4. Today we come to take a decision of faith commitment.

READING THE SIGNS OF THE TIMES

5. We have heard that creation continues to groan, in bondage, waiting for its liberation (Rom 8.22). We are challenged by the cries of the people who suffer and by the woundedness of creation itself. We see a dramatic convergence between the suffering of the people and the damage done to the rest of creation.

6. The signs of the times have become more alarming and must be interpreted. The root causes of massive threats to life are above all the product of an unjust economic system defended and protected by political and military might. Economic systems are a matter of life or death.

7. We live in a scandalous world that denies God's call to life for all. The annual income of the richest 1 percent is equal to that of the poorest 57 percent, and 24,000 people die each day from poverty and malnutrition. The debt of poor countries continues to increase despite paying back their original borrowing many times over. Resource-driven wars claim the lives of millions, while millions more die of preventable diseases. The HIV and AIDS global pandemic afflicts life in all parts of the world, affecting the poorest where generic drugs are not available. The majority of those in poverty are women and children and the number of people living in absolute poverty on less than one US dollar per day continues to increase.

8. The policy of unlimited growth among industrialized countries and the drive for profit of transnational corporations have plundered the earth and severely damaged the environment. In 1989, one species disappeared each day, and by 2000 it was one every hour. Climate change, the depletion of fish stocks, deforestation, soil erosion, and threats to fresh water are among the devastating consequences. Communities are disrupted, livelihoods are lost, coastal regions and Pacific islands are threatened with inundation, and storms increase. High levels of radioactivity threaten health and ecology. Life forms and cultural knowledge are being patented for financial gain.

9. This crisis is directly related to the development of neoliberal economic globalization, which is based on the following beliefs:

- unrestrained competition, consumerism, and the unlimited economic growth and accumulation of wealth is the best for the whole world;
- the ownership of private property has no social obligation;
- capital speculation, liberalization and deregulation of the market, privatization of public utilities and national resources, unrestricted access for foreign investments and imports, lower taxes, and the unrestricted movement of capital will achieve wealth for all;
- social obligations, protection of the poor and the weak, trade unions, and relationships between people are subordinate to the processes of economic growth and capital accumulation.

10. This is an ideology that claims to be without alternative, demanding an endless flow of sacrifices from the poor and creation. It makes the false promise that it can save the world through the creation of wealth and prosperity, claiming sovereignty over life and demanding total allegiance, which amounts to idolatry.

11. We recognize the enormity and complexity of the situation. We do not seek simple answers. As seekers of truth and justice and looking through the eyes of powerless and suffering people, we see that the current world (dis)order is rooted in an extremely complex and immoral economic system defended by empire. In using the term "empire" we mean the coming together of economic, cultural, political and military power that constitutes a system of domination led by powerful nations to protect and defend their own interests.

12. In classical liberal economics, the state exists to protect private property and contracts in the competitive market. Through the struggles of the labour movement, states began to regulate markets and provide for the welfare of people. Since the 1980s, through the transnationalization of capital, neoliberalism has set out to dismantle the welfare functions of the state. Under neoliberalism the purpose of the economy is to increase profits and return for the owners of production and financial capital, while excluding the majority of the people and treating nature as a commodity.

13. As markets have become global, so have the political and legal institutions which protect them. The government of the United States of America and its allies, together with international finance and trade institutions (International Monetary Fund, World Bank, World Trade Organization) use political, economic, or military alliances to protect and advance the interest of capital owners.

14. We see the dramatic convergence of the economic crisis with the integration of economic globalization and geopolitics backed by neoliberal ideology. This is a global system that defends and protects the interests of the powerful. It affects and captivates us all. Further, in biblical terms such a system of wealth accumulation at the expense of the poor is seen as unfaithful to God and responsible for preventable human suffering and is called Mammon. Jesus has told us that we cannot serve both God and Mammon (Lk 16.13).

CONFESSION OF FAITH IN THE FACE OF ECONOMIC INJUSTICE AND ECOLOGICAL DESTRUCTION

15. Faith commitment may be expressed in various ways according to regional and theological traditions: as confession, as confessing together, as faith stance, as being faithful to the covenant of God. We choose confession, not meaning a classical doctrinal confession, because the World Alliance of Reformed Churches cannot make such a confession, but to show the necessity and urgency of an active response to the challenges of our time and the call of Debrecen. We invite member churches to receive and respond to our common witness.

16. Speaking from our Reformed tradition and having read the signs of the times, the General Council of the World Alliance of Reformed Churches affirms that global economic justice is essential to the integrity of our faith in God and our discipleship as Christians. We believe that the integrity of our faith is at stake if we remain silent or refuse to act in the face of the current system of neoliberal economic globalization and therefore we confess before God and one another.

17. We believe in God, Creator and Sustainer of all life, who calls us as partners in the creation and redemption of the world. We live under the promise that Jesus Christ came so that all might have life in fullness (Jn 10.10). Guided and upheld by the Holy Spirit we open ourselves to the reality of our world.

18. We believe that God is sovereign over all creation. "The earth is the Lord's and the fullness thereof" (Ps 24.1).

19. Therefore, we reject the current world economic order imposed by global neoliberal capitalism and any other economic system, including absolute planned economies, which defy God's covenant by excluding the poor, the vulnerable and the whole of creation from the fullness of life. We reject any claim of economic, political, and military empire which subverts God's sovereignty over life and acts contrary to God's just rule.

20. We believe that God has made a covenant with all of creation (Gen 9.8–12). God has brought into being an earth community based on the vision of justice and peace. The covenant is a gift of grace that is not for sale in the market place (Is 55.1). It is an economy of grace for the household of all of creation. Jesus shows that this is an inclusive covenant in which the poor and marginalized are preferential partners, and calls us to put justice for the "least of these" (Mt 25.40) at the centre of the community of life. All creation is blessed and included in this covenant (Hos 2.18ff).

21. Therefore we reject the culture of rampant consumerism and the competitive greed and selfishness of the neoliberal global market system, or any other system, which claims there is no alternative.

22. We believe that any economy of the household of life, given to us by God's covenant to sustain life, is accountable to God. We believe the economy exists

to serve the dignity and well-being of people in community, within the bounds of the sustainability of creation. We believe that human beings are called to choose God over Mammon and that confessing our faith is an act of obedience.

23. Therefore we reject the unregulated accumulation of wealth and limitless growth that has already cost the lives of millions and destroyed much of God's creation.

24. We believe that God is a God of justice. In a world of corruption, exploitation, and greed, God is in a special way the God of the destitute, the poor, the exploited, the wronged, and the abused (Ps 146.7–9). God calls for just relationships with all creation.

25. Therefore we reject any ideology or economic regime that puts profits before people, does not care for all creation, and privatizes those gifts of God meant for all. We reject any teaching which justifies those who support, or fail to resist, such an ideology in the name of the gospel.

26. We believe that God calls us to stand with those who are victims of injustice. We know what the Lord requires of us: to do justice, love kindness, and walk in God's way (Mic 6.8). We are called to stand against any form of injustice in the economy and the destruction of the environment, "so that justice may roll down like waters, and righteousness like an ever-flowing stream" (Amos 5.24).

27. Therefore we reject any theology that claims that God is only with the rich and that poverty is the fault of the poor. We reject any form of injustice which destroys right relations—gender, race, class, disability, or caste. We reject any theology which affirms that human interests dominate nature.

28. We believe that God calls us to hear the cries of the poor and the groaning of creation and to follow the public mission of Jesus Christ who came so that all may have life and have it in fullness (Jn 10.10). Jesus brings justice to the oppressed and gives bread to the hungry; he frees the prisoner and restores sight to the blind (Lk 4.18); he supports and protects the downtrodden, the stranger, the orphans and the widows.

29. Therefore we reject any church practice or teaching which excludes the poor and care for creation, in its mission; giving comfort to those who come to "steal, kill and destroy" (Jn 10.10) rather than following the "Good Shepherd" who has come for life for all (Jn 10.11).

30. We believe that God calls men, women and children from every place together, rich and poor, to uphold the unity of the church and its mission, so that the reconciliation to which Christ calls can become visible.

31. Therefore we reject any attempt in the life of the church to separate justice and unity.

32. We believe that we are called in the Spirit to account for the hope that is within us through Jesus Christ, and believe that justice shall prevail and peace shall reign.

33. We commit ourselves to seek a global covenant for justice in the economy and the earth in the household of God.

34. We humbly confess this hope, knowing that we, too, stand under the judgement of God's justice.

- We acknowledge the complicity and guilt of those who consciously or unconsciously benefit from the current neoliberal economic global system; we recognize that this includes both churches and members of our own Reformed family and therefore we call for confession of sin.
- We acknowledge that we have become captivated by the culture of consumerism, and the competitive greed and selfishness of the current economic system. This has all too often permeated our very spirituality.
- We confess our sin in misusing creation and failing to play our role as stewards and companions of nature.
- We confess our sin that our disunity within the Reformed family has impaired our ability to serve God's mission in fullness.

35. We believe, in obedience to Jesus Christ, that the church is called to confess, witness and act, even though the authorities and human law might forbid them, and punishment and suffering be the consequence (Acts 4.18ff). Jesus is Lord.

36. We join in praise to God, Creator, Redeemer, Spirit, who has "brought down the mighty from their thrones, lifted up the lowly, filled the hungry with good things and sent the rich away with empty hands" (Lk 1.52f).

COVENANTING FOR JUSTICE

37. By confessing our faith together, we covenant in obedience to God's will as an act of faithfulness in mutual solidarity and in accountable relationships. This binds us together to work for justice in the economy and the earth both in our common global context as well as our various regional and local settings.

38. On this common journey, some churches have already expressed their commitment in a confession of faith. We urge them to continue to translate this confession into concrete actions both regionally and locally. Other churches have already begun to engage in this process, including taking actions and we urge them to engage further, through education, confession and action. To those other churches, which are still in the process of recognition, we urge them on the basis of our mutual covenanting accountability, to deepen their education and move forward towards confession.

39. The General Council calls upon member churches, on the basis of this covenanting relationship, to undertake the difficult and prophetic task of interpreting this confession to their local congregations.

40. The General Council urges member churches to implement this confession by following up the Public Issues Committee's recommendations on economic justice and ecological issues.

41. The General Council commits the World Alliance of Reformed Churches to work together with other communions, the ecumenical community, the community of other faiths, civil movements and people's movements for a just economy and the integrity of creation and calls upon our member churches to do the same.

42. Now we proclaim with passion that we will commit ourselves, our time and our energy to changing, renewing, and restoring the economy and the earth, choosing life, so that we and our descendants might live (Deut 30.19).

Glossary

Christian realism School of thought associated with Reinhold Niebuhr (1892–1971). Christian realism sought to formulate a new liberal theology on a more "realistic" basis that took seriously the limitations of human beings to overcome sin and evil.

Deliberative democracy A model for decision making on political issues that encourages decisions to be made by consensus and full representation, and which places the power upon smaller groups working together to envision creative proposals for change.

Ecumenical The Greek root of this term, *oikoumene*, literally means "the whole inhabited earth." The term "ecumenical" refers to the concern for cooperation among Christians and is often used in reference to movements that foster Christian unity.

Empire The direct dominion of a sovereign nation over conquered peoples and their territories.

Enlightenment A period in eighteenth-century Europe marked by significant shifts in philosophical and scientific methodologies. New methods emerging at that time questioned the authority of the church and the clergy as the primary source of truth and emphasized human reason as the means to pursue truth.

Globalization Process by which people, nations, and economies throughout the world become ever more connected and integrated. Although often driven by economics, globalization includes cultural, political, and human welfare dimensions.

Imperialism The policy of extending the rule or authority of one nation over another, either through the expansion of one nation's territory or through economic or political policies that significantly impact another nation.

Liberal theology A theological movement that developed in the nineteenth and twentieth centuries, marked by a dual emphasis on reason, science, and experience as sources of knowledge while affirming the sovereignty and divinity of Christ and the relevance of Christian faith and traditions for contemporary concerns.

Liberation theology Theological movements beginning in the twentieth century that see Christianity's central message as liberation from all forms of political, economic, and social oppression.

Mainline denomination A term used to describe Protestant churches that have historically been influential in the shaping of American religious life.

Militarism Term used in Christian ethics to underscore an excessive exaltation of war, martial values, and the military establishment.

Normative claims In ethics, claims intended to establish guidelines or standards to guide behavior and actions.

Postmodernism The philosophical view that our contemporary intellectual and cultural climate has moved beyond the modernism introduced by the Enlightenment. Postmodernists reject the idea that universal and objective claims to truth can be made.

Principle A general truth or rule that functions as a fundamental assumption undergirding ethical action.

Progressive Christianity In this book, progressive Christianity is used to describe an understanding of Christian tradition marked by an awareness of social sin, a consciousness of institutional and human potential and shortcomings, and an emphasis on the church's mission to engage the world.

Public education A tuition-free, publicly funded system that must provide an education to each child in a neighborhood school within a publicly governed school system. The academic standards, the teachers and administrators, and the values and methods of operation employed in these schools are all subject to oversight and direction by public policy-making bodies. The rights of students and parents are legally defined and enforceable by the courts.

Public policy Generally defined as a system of laws, regulatory measures, courses of action, and funding priorities concerning a given topic promulgated by a governmental entity or its representatives.

Social Gospel movement A Christian movement beginning in the late nineteenth and early twentieth centuries that sought to respond to economic and social disparities created by increased industrialization.

Index